HARD CASH

A Primer for the Small Investor

by

Philip L. Groves

Strebor Publications

Laguna Beach, California

Published by Strebor Publications, P. O. Box 475, Laguna Beach, CA 92652

First Printing March 1994

Cover Illustration by Philip L. Groves, Jr.

Library of Congress Catalog Number 93-86816

Groves, Philip L.

HARD CASH: A Primer for the Small Investor

ISBN 0-9629498-3-3

Printed in the United States of America

DEDICATION

To Patsy, for her patience, and to those would-be investors who just want to know the time of day, not how a watch is made.

TABLE OF CONTENTS

LIST OF APPENDICES

INTRODUCTION

This little book is for people who don't know the difference between a stock and a baseball bat and really don't want to know much more. It's also for people who have a little money, say $5,000, in a savings account or CD and are afraid to do anything "risky" because their neighbor, sister, or son-in-law lost thousands after buying some stock, bond, or mutual fund. It's for people who were sold an investment they didn't understand, and when its market value dropped, they panicked and sold out just before it went back up. And finally, it's for people who lack an objective friend or relative who is also an experienced and successful investor. If you can identify with any of the above, read on.

There are many ways to lose money while engaged in what some may call investing, but which in reality is only gambling. For instance, it's gambling when you buy without first setting down a long-range investment plan. It's gambling when you buy into a program that has no performance history or track record. You're gambling when you attempt to trade in individual stocks, bonds, or commodities without doing substantial research first, and then having the staying power—the money—to be able to add to or subtract from those positions as conditions dictate.

It comes as a mild shock to many when they learn that the typical dabbler in the stock market will, over the course of several years, be lucky to break even. Amateur option traders fare much worse, and about ninety percent of the beginners who trade commodity futures contracts quickly lose all of their investment.

Successful investing, on the other hand, can be as simple as structuring a portfolio of mutual funds which fit your personal situation. In Section II, I will talk about how to do that in three easy steps. In other sections, I will discuss the following:

1) Risk factors you can and cannot control
2) Picking your own stocks and bonds
3) IRA accounts and limited partnerships

In short, my goal is to start you in a direction in which you will have a good chance of making a decent return on your hard-earned money—without the help of a stockbroker or financial planner—and still sleep at night. After which, maybe a few of you will be stimulated to search beyond the limited scope of this primer to uncover more sophisticated aspects of securities investing.

If you are already a frequent reader of investment articles found in such magazines as *Business Week, Consumer Reports, Forbes,* and *Money,* to name a few, you will find little new in this book—especially where mutual funds are discussed. In that case, feel free to recommend it to a friend. If, however, you are among the thousands of folks who crave a simple investment guide to getting started—not a text book—you may turn the page.

I

RISK - IT'S THE "PRINCIPAL" OF THE THING

Starting an investment program can be a little like getting in line for your first roller coaster ride. You don't really know what it's going to be like until you actually do it. However, there is one big difference: With roller coaster riding you make a total commitment—there is no such thing as getting off in the middle. With conservative investing, on the other hand, you can limit your money commitment to your personal comfort level, and easily get out if or when you've had enough.

So while it's difficult to establish your "risk tolerance" in advance, you *can* build a portfolio which will be unlikely to surprise you with either catastrophic losses or exhilarating profits. If it's able to provide an average annual return which consistently outpaces inflation by ten percentage points, you should be very happy.

Such a portfolio does not happen by accident. However, the recipe for controlling much of the risk is a simple one which I will reveal shortly. In the meantime, it may help to learn a little about some risk factors you *cannot* control, but which will influence the overall performance of your program:

Inflation erodes the future buying power of your savings. It happens when the dollar is worth less to a Japanese automaker than it was last year, when there aren't enough paid parking spaces in your building to go around, or when the cost of twigs for building wicker furniture goes up.

So whatever you do, your portfolio—all your investments taken together—has to generate a return at least equal to the rate of inflation or you'll go backwards. At a 5% annual inflation rate, idle cash will lose over half its buying power in fifteen years. But like most things in life, inflation seldom stays at a steady pace for long. In 1980 it hit 13.5%. As of this writing (1993) the rate is about 3%.

If the past sixty some years are any indicator of what the future may hold, common stocks will continue to outpace inflation better than any other type of investment. According to *Fidelity Focus*—Summer 1993, The Standard & Poor's 500 Stock Price Index (S&P 500) has returned—dividends reinvested—an average of over ten percent per year since 1926. That's almost double the average return for long-term corporate bonds, and almost triple the rate for U.S. Treasury bills. Over the same time, the annual rate of inflation has averaged about three percent.

Of course, the average investor couldn't afford to buy all 500 stocks that make up the S&P 500 index. This and other indexes are used here only as a basis for comparison.

So, what does it mean in dollars and cents? Let's go back to 1926 and **simulate** an investment of $1,000 each in the S&P 500 index, long-term corporate bonds, and short-term U.S. Treasury bills—reinvest dividends and interest—and see what those purchases were worth by 1993. For simplicity's sake, we'll leave out Uncle Sam's tax bite in the illustration which follows:

	1926	**Annual return**	**1993**
S&P 500	$1,000	10.20%	$670,142
Corporate bonds	$1,000	5.50%	$ 36,134
Treasury bills	$1,000	3.75%	$ 11,782

Keep in mind a couple of things: Over that sixty-seven year period, the S&P 500 had nineteen **down** years. That averages about three down years in every ten. And to just keep up with inflation from 1926 until 1993, $1,000 had to grow to $7,733.

Interest Rates determine what it costs you to rent (borrow) money or, conversely, what you earn when you rent (lend) money to someone else. When you buy bonds, you're lending money to either Uncle Sam, a corporation, or a municipality which promises to pay you periodic interest at, usually, a fixed rate. They also promise that, at some pre-established time in the future (the maturity date), they will pay you back the amount printed on the bond (the face amount—the principal). If, in the meantime, interest rates go up, the bonds in your portfolio will drop in market value because the rate they are paying isn't as attractive as the new rate. The opposite is true if rates go down—your bonds will go up in value. In either case however, the periodic interest payments to you will not change. That's why they're called **fixed-income** securities. Money market mutual funds behave the other way around. The price stays fixed at a dollar per share while the interest payment changes daily. That's because the securities in the fund have very short maturities so their prices vary only slightly.

As for stocks, the effect will vary with the type of stock and the industry of the company that the stock represents. As a shareholder—part owner—your concern should be the long-term growth prospects of the company. However, many investors holding stocks paying high quarterly dividends tend to compare their dividend income with bond yields, and these investors can affect market prices by shifting back and forth between stocks and bonds with the interest rate tide.

Market & Economic factors often set the psychological tone for what happens next to the price of stocks, bonds, etc. Here, self-fulfilling prophecies abound: When enough people only *think* something will happen—like a recession—it often does whether it needed to or not. Furthermore, the effect on stock and bond prices can be just the opposite of what you might have predicted. In a falling stock market, there are always some stocks that go up, some that stay even, and some that don't go down very much. That's because what is often referred to as "the market" is a group of only thirty stocks making up the Dow Jones Industrial Average. While those few blue chip stocks do influence the direction of prices, remember there are over five-thousand other stocks being traded on various exchanges and over-the-counter, and many of them just do their own thing.

Finally, since few professional economists ever agree on either where the economy is headed or its effect on the various markets, it is futile for the layman to try to make investment decisions based on market or economic forecasts. Besides, economists are always "revising" their predictions as new information emerges—so they're seldom right or wrong for very long. In the meantime, you could be stuck with whatever buy or sell decision you made after reading their original version.

Business Management factors are the consequences of executive decision making. What corporate leaders seem to be doing about their competition, changes in demand for their products, or policies of the government will most certainly have some effect on the price of the underlying stocks. In addition, bookkeeping practices, not readily apparent, could either understate or overstate the value of certain corporate assets. Once correctly perceived by the market, the price of the stock could change significantly.

The above risk factors all interact with each other in sometimes complex ways: Well-informed large investors who foresee the rate of inflation increasing will demand higher interest payments—yields—before buying long-term bonds. This action will cause the price of existing bonds to fall. Also, signs of economic change or uncertainty may cause many professionals to either buy, sell, or go to the sidelines to wait for things to clear up. Unfortunately, by the time these and other perceptions reach you, the small investor, in the form of newspaper and magazine articles, or even through your stockbroker, it may be too late to lock-in a profit or avoid a loss.

Now, since you can't control inflation, interest rates, markets, and so forth, what can you do? At the beginning of this section, I promised a simple recipe for containing risk: Its main ingredient is **history**. Although it's a fact that history is not a reliable predictor of the future price of a stock, bond, or whatever, it does provide a reliable forecast of their **volatility**. Stocks, even mutual funds, which have a history of large and frequent price swings will, with few exceptions, behave likewise into the future.

It's also true that although investors are, in the long run, rewarded for taking on greater risk (higher volatility), the rewards are seldom in-line-with the additional risk, after a certain point. In other words, a moderate increase in risk will, in the long run, produce a moderate increase in profits, but a great increase in risk will probably give no better than a moderate return, and may do even worse.

While it may seem a little too pat to be credible, by simply selecting a portfolio of stocks, or stock mutual funds with the same volatility as a broad market index, say the S&P 500, investors may reasonably expect a level of performance close to that index. A so-called "index mutual fund" does just that by buying *all* the stocks making up the index.

Consistently achieving that level of performance wouldn't be all bad considering many professional portfolio managers, including those seeking to exceed it, are unable to do so. On the other hand, many such managers are able to produce far better results than the average small investor can—with or without the help of a stockbroker or financial advisor.

We'll talk about how to hire a professional portfolio manager in the section on mutual funds—next.

II

MUTUAL FUNDS - WELL NOTHING'S PERFECT

Mutual Fund is the popular name for an investment company whose sole purpose in life is to profitably manage a portfolio of assorted securities. Depending on the investment objectives of the company, the portfolio may include stocks, bonds, options, real estate, commodities, or a combination of things—for example, stocks and bonds.

When you buy a mutual fund, you are acquiring shares in their securities holdings, and, in effect, hiring a portfolio manager or team of managers to do any trading on your behalf. As part owner of a portfolio worth many millions of dollars, you will share in the capital gains (losses), dividends, and interest income the fund may generate.

Unless you plan to pay a stockbroker or financial planner a commission to help you select a fund or funds, the cost to own them can be quite low. The yearly management fees and expenses charged by many excellent funds are less than one percent of the total dollars invested. And because a well-established fund buys and sells securities in large quantities, they also pay low commissions to their brokers—and that savings is passed on to you.

On the other hand, a wealthy investor who hires a private portfolio manager frequently pays two, sometimes three percent per year plus a "performance" fee if the manager does better than average. In addition, unless the management company controls a very large sum of money, it will pay higher brokerage commissions. Obviously, it would be hard to justify staying with a private portfolio manager whose track record for performance is not consistently superior to that of mutual funds with similar objectives. Besides, the minimum investment required by a well-established money manager is seldom less than a quarter million dollars. You can get into many mutual funds for a thousand dollars—some for even less.

Of the almost four thousand mutual funds around, most are open-end companies. They're called that because they can keep issuing shares as long as there are willing buyers. And, as you might have guessed, there are closed-end companies—a few hundred—which issue a fixed number of shares. They trade on exchanges or over-the-counter, like individual stocks. For now, we'll deal only with the open-end variety.

Among the open-end companies are so-called LOAD, LOW-LOAD, and NO-LOAD funds. The load is the sales charge—the commission—which can range from 1% to 8.5%. Since you ought to be making your own selections, you should buy only no-load or low-load funds directly from the investment companies themselves. While upfront sales charges are the most visible entry costs of a load fund, even some no-load funds have exit and/or marketing fees that are not so conspicuous. We'll cover how to avoid these and other hidden charges later.

Although there is a dazzling variety of mutual funds available today—enough to paralyze many novice investors from doing anything—we will deal with only the following types:

1) MONEY MARKET: Short-term (liquid) debt instruments

2)   GROWTH: Mostly stocks (maximum, international, etc.)

3)   INCOME: Mostly bonds (mid-term, tax-exempt, etc.)

4)   GROWTH & INCOME: Mostly stocks paying high dividends

As the section heading suggests, mutual funds are not perfect, but they can provide an excellent savings growth opportunity for the small investor. The investment decisions are left to the full-time professionals running the funds, and you—the shareholder—can truly participate in the rewards and be out fishing at the same time.

In the Introduction, I promised a three-step plan for building a portfolio of mutual funds. While the following is not a breakthrough in investment planning, it is simple and thus a good way to start a program:

STEP 1.   Establish A Time Horizon For Your Program

STEP 2.   Make A Pie Chart Of Your Portfolio

STEP 3.   Select The Best Mutual Funds To Fit the Chart

STEP 1: Establish a time horizon at that point in the future when you plan to convert your portfolio to cash. It may be to start a business, to fund a child's education, or to shift to a conservative retirement program. Basically, the more time you have to get there, the more risk you can take along the way. For the very long-term program, say from the early-career stage of your life to your retirement, you should make at least three structural changes to your

portfolio before reaching your time horizon.   Each
subsequent stage should be more conservative than the
previous one. For example:

STAGE OF LIFE	ACTION	PORTFOLIO OBJECTIVE
Early Career	Start with	Aggressive Growth
Mid Career	Switch to	Moderate Growth
Late Career	Switch to	Growth & Income
Early Retirement	Switch to	Conservative Growth & Income
Late Retirement	Switch to	Conservative Income

Naturally, if you're not able to begin your program until,
say, Late Career, then your portfolio objective should start
with Growth & Income. Just remember that when you get
within three or so years of the time horizon, you should
move towards an ultra conservative posture such as money
market funds, CDs, or Treasury bills. This allows you to
protect your gains from eleventh-hour losses when there's
no time to recoup.

Finally, many investors establish more than one time
horizon depending on how much they can save and when
certain events are expected to occur. For example, you
might plan to start your own business in ten years, fund a
child's college in fifteen, and retire in thirty.

STEP 2: Make a pie chart of investments which are
suitable for your time horizon. This "portfolio approach"
has two major benefits:

1) It forces you to allocate funds where the risks are appropriate for your stage of life.

2) It helps you keep the "big picture" in mind as market values fluctuate—when one part of your portfolio goes down, another part may not drop as much, and still another may even go up.

The pie charts shown at the end of this chapter suggest a conservative allocation of mutual funds to go with the five life stages mentioned above. Except for "Utilities," avoid, for now, the temptation to venture into the so-called sector funds such as "technology," "small company," "precious metals," etc. Doing so may result in my earlier roller coaster analogy coming to life.

STEP 3. Select the best mutual funds to fit your pie chart, and begin a systematic purchase schedule. There are a number of sources of mutual fund performance data to help you make the best picks. Some are in the form of expensive newsletters which provide frequent—too frequent—updates of prices and rankings. Of course the fund prospectus (the official offering document) must be reviewed before buying, and though some are written in plain cnglish, many are better used as a cure for insomnia.

The least expensive and easiest to understand sources of information are found at any newsstand among the business and consumer magazines. Among those which issue at least an annual mutual fund report are:

TITLE	SPECIAL FEATURE
Business Week	Three or ten-year trend graphic
Consumer Reports	Results: $2000 per yr for 5 yrs
Forbes	ABCDF risk-adjusted ranking
Money	% gain (loss) in up/down markets

Most annual mutual fund reports are published in February to reflect the previous January through December performance data. These reports are often followed by updates throughout the year. If nothing is on the magazine racks now, then visit your downtown library. They should have back-issues on special shelves or on microfilm. Where mutual funds are concerned, reports several months old will suffice to get you started.

Avoid making a buy or sell decision based on a ranking report that covers short time periods such as: "the top-ten funds of the month" or "...the quarter." A fund with an excellent long-term track record may make the top-ten for April, and disappear from that category in May. Such an event would seldom be a reason to panic and sell, but may in fact be a buying opportunity—after further analysis.

Also, don't be confused by the fact that one magazine's rankings will differ from another's. They each use slightly different formulas for establishing risk. Some rank funds after adjusting for risk while others disclose the risk but rank from the highest "total returns" on down. If possible, review all the reports. If that's too much like work or confusing, then settle on the magazine which seems easiest for you. Whichever you choose, they all list the phone numbers, usually toll-free, for ordering the fund prospectus and application forms.

Before sending off for a bunch of literature, however, let's discuss the selection process and how to narrow the list from several hundred down to one. It's done by, of all things, the process of elimination. Let's say you're looking for the best long-term GROWTH fund for your Early Career pie chart. Most magazines which publish annual mutual fund reports will rank the top performing funds by type—investment objective. In that case, stick with the top-performing funds labeled GROWTH. Then **eliminate** those funds which:

1) Have less than a ten-year track record

2) Have a sales charge (load) above 2% (front-end/back-end)

3) Charge "Rule 12(b)-1" fee

4) Have expense ratio in excess of 1.5%

5) Are ranked HIGH in "turnover" (trading activity)

6) Are ranked HIGH in risk

True, this is a very conservative approach. Many excellent funds may have one or more of the above features, but you should uncover some compelling performance results before picking them. If that seems like too much trouble, the above analysis should reveal two or three good choices. At this point, look at the one with the highest *Total Return* over the last ten years. If it also compares well over the past three-year and five-year periods, it's probably a good choice. If it doesn't, then look at the next best performer, and so on. Or you can always skip the last two steps and just employ the classic selection process: Enie, Meany, Miney, Moe.

Total Return is the best single indicator of fund performance, regardless of type. You may also see performance stated as the Average Annual Return, or Compounded Annual Return. However stated, it should represent the net gain to the investor after reinvesting dividends and capital gains in additional shares of the fund. Even if you plan to take your dividends in cash—to supplement a pension, for example—the total return figure provides the best apples and apples comparison. Many so-called High-Yield Government Bond mutual funds may pay very high "distribution rates," but part of the distribution probably includes a return of principal from mortgages that were paid off early. Such a fund would not do well when comparing total returns, but would look good when comparing "distribution rates"—sometimes incorrectly referred to as **yield**. While bond portfolio managers may generate additional income with various strategies designed to protect (hedge) their holdings, "yield" can only come from the interest paid by the bonds themselves.

If the prospect of comparing total return, risk, turnover, and so forth, seems too daunting and time consuming, then just pick the #1 ranked fund from the appropriate type for your pie chart and be done with it. Just remember that often the effect of any sales charge is not deducted from the published performance figures. So, if that #1 fund happens to have a 8.5% sales charge, the value of a $5,000 investment ($4,575 after the sales charge) which averaged 15% total return per year for 10 years would be $18,508. The same performance with a no-load fund (all $5,000 invested) would be $20,228. You decide.

Once you've chosen the funds to match your pie chart, dial the toll-free numbers of their distributors (found in the report) and order the prospectuses and application forms.

Once received, review each prospectus—it gets easier with practice. Next, complete the application forms. In this example, Early Career, you would indicate that all distributions from dividends and capital gains be reinvested in additional shares of the fund. Later, when you reach the retirement stage, you will have switched from growth to mostly income funds—at which point you may want to have the monthly dividends paid-out to you in cash. Just a note here about taxes: whether you take the dividends in cash or reinvest them, Uncle Sam will want his share of tax dollars each year that the fund makes a distribution. Also, whenever you sell your shares, hopefully at a profit, he will want to tax any gains which you haven't already paid taxes on along the way. This will not become a problem if you carefully file all account statements for future reference. Of course, any funds which are part of a retirement account, such as an IRA or 401(k), are tax-deferred until you start taking cash distributions.

If, for example, you have a total of $5,000 to invest, then your Early Career pie chart calls for 30% or $1,500 in a long-term growth fund. So send your check for that amount along with the completed application form to the fund. If it's a no-load fund and its net-asset-value (NAV) is, say, $17.23 per share when your check arrives, you will be the proud owner of 87.057 shares. If it's a load fund with a 5.5% sales charge, then the offering price will be $18.23 and you will be the slightly less-proud owner of 82.282 shares. See Appendix A for the calculations.

The ability to buy fractional shares (82.282) is a key feature when the time comes to reinvest distributions, because every penny goes into the additional shares. When you hold a position for the long-term, while reinvesting all dividends and capital gains in more fund shares, ten years later the NAV of the fund could be unchanged, but the value of your position might have quadrupled.

In contrast, the opportunity for the small investor to reinvest dividends with a portfolio of individual stocks, while possible, is greatly limited. Most either spend their cash dividends or reinvest them in a [low-yielding] money market fund. Please note: reinvesting distributions in additional shares is not possible if you take delivery of a mutual fund's certificate. So let the funds—in effect—hold the certificates in safekeeping, and send you periodic statements instead.

Because any success by most small investors in correctly timing the market can best be credited to luck, the old-faithful principle of **Dollar-Cost-Averaging** should be employed instead. Simply put, it is a method for investing the same amount of money each month, or each quarter, or whatever regular period suits your situation. By doing so over the long haul of up and down markets, you are more likely to lower your average cost per share when compared to making infrequent lump-sum purchases. After making the initial minimum investment ($1,000 to $3,000), most funds allow additions of as little as twenty-five dollars at a time. Just keep in mind your original pie chart when adding to your fund positions—to keep them in proportion.

Once you've established your portfolio, the process of evaluating its performance is similar to what you did during the initial selection process. You compare a growth (stock) portfolio to a widely accepted index such as the S&P 500, and you compare an income (bond) portfolio to, say, the Lehman Brothers Government/Corporate Bond or Municipal Bond Indexes. Also, compare results with other funds of similar type.

It's important to exercise patience, however, and let the professionals you hired, through the purchase of the funds, do their work. If after two or three years, one or more of your funds has not lived up to reasonable expectations, then carefully consider switching. Just bear in mind that more than a few investors have sold Fund A just before it started back up, only to replace it with Fund B just before it dropped in value.

While account statements vary among investment companies, they all either display your fund's performance for the period or contain the figures so that you can make the calculations yourself. Some of the large funds have a computerized toll-free telephone service which provides complete information on your account's value—24 hours a day. And, of course, you can get a handle on share prices under the Mutual Funds section of the newspaper.

Using our Early Career example and some make-believe funds, on the following page let's evaluate each fund as well as the portfolio as a whole for the year 1989—a year when the S&P 500 went up 31.7%.

Note: In the following table, the INITIAL INVESTMENT column represents purchases made January 1; YEAR-END VALUE column indicates total shares in each fund, including those added by reinvesting dividends and capital gains.

Now, let's take a look at the table on the following page:

SAMPLE EARLY CAREER PORTFOLIO

MUTUAL FUND (Allocation)	INITIAL INVESTMENT	YEAR-END VALUE (No. Shares x NAV)	TOTAL RETURN*
Money Market (20%)	$1000	1082 x $ 1.0 = $1082.00	8.2%
International Growth (15%)	$ 750	44.4 x $21.5 = $ 954.60	27.3%
Long Term Growth (30%)	$1500	134.1 x $13.3 = $1783.53	18.9%
Maximum Growth (35%)	$1750	39.3 x $58.9 = $2314.77	32.3%
TOTALS (100%)	$5000	$6134.90	22.7%

*Total Return = (Gain / Initial Investment) x 100; Gain = 6134.90 — 5000 = 1134.90
                  = (1134.90 / 5000) x 100 = 22.7%

Now, you may quibble, that's only 22.7% versus 31.7% for the S&P 500. But remember, if you can outpace inflation by ten percentage points, you should be happy. In 1989, the inflation rate averaged just under 5%. At 22.7%, our make-believe portfolio is 17.7 percentage points above that. Not bad. Also keep in mind that 50% of the portfolio is made up of a low volatility growth fund and a money market fund. That combination will act as a protective hedge against the inevitable market downturns.

Of course, 1989 was a very good year for many stocks. Over the past five years, 1988-1993, our make-believe portfolio could have averaged 14% per year—with the international growth fund dragging things down a bit. Over that same period, inflation has averaged less than 4% a year, and the S&P 500 averaged 16.1% per year.

Although it's a mistake to constantly check the paper for market prices on the funds in your portfolio—it'll just make you nervous—you'll probably want to evaluate your holdings more frequently than once a year. The calculation for measuring performance when you are adding or withdrawing money from the portfolio is complicated, and the periodic statements sent to you by the funds won't tell the whole story. So, I've included a simplified process which yields an approximate figure in Appendix C.

If, at this point, your thirst for investment knowledge remains unquenched, some ideas for picking your own stocks and bonds are given in Chapter III which follows the pie charts on the following pages.

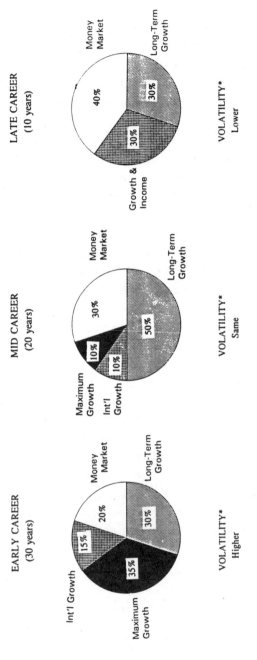

ALLOCATION OF MUTUAL FUNDS

STAGE OF LIFE (Time Horizon) FOR EACH CHART AS SHOWN

EARLY CAREER
(30 years)

- Money Market — 20%
- Int'l Growth — 15%
- Long-Term Growth — 30%
- Maximum Growth — 35%

VOLATILITY*
Higher

MID CAREER
(20 years)

- Money Market — 30%
- Maximum Growth — 10%
- Int'l Growth — 10%
- Long-Term Growth — 50%

VOLATILITY*
Same

LATE CAREER
(10 years)

- Money Market — 40%
- Long-Term Growth — 30%
- Growth & Income — 30%

VOLATILITY*
Lower

*VOLATILITY VS. S&P 500

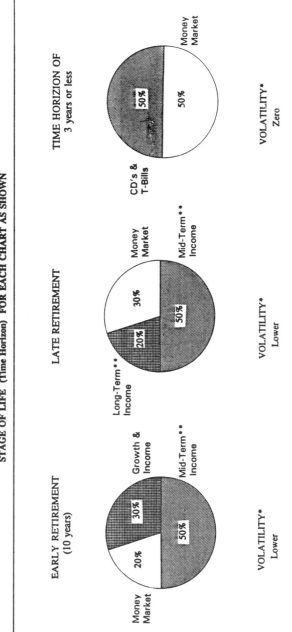

ALLOCATION OF MUTUAL FUNDS

STAGE OF LIFE (Time Horizon) FOR EACH CHART AS SHOWN

TIME HORIZION OF
3 years or less

Money Market

CD's & T-Bills

50%

50%

VOLATILITY*
Zero

LATE RETIREMENT

Money Market

Mid-Term** Income

Long-Term** Income

30%

20%

50%

VOLATILITY*
Lower

EARLY RETIREMENT
(10 years)

Growth & Income

Mid-Term** Income

Money Market

30%

20%

50%

VOLATILITY*
Lower

*VOLATILITY VS. S&P 500

**Select taxable or tax-exempt funds depending on tax bracket.

NOTES

III

SO YOU STILL WANT TO PICK YOUR OWN STOCKS & BONDS

Before Peter Lynch retired from his post as manager of the top-ranked **Fidelity Magellan** mutual fund, he worked six and seven day weeks researching company reports and visiting the executives of hundreds of corporations. He seldom read a newspaper or spent time with his family. No doubt his workaholic approach to picking stocks accounted, in large measure, for the superior track record of the fund—up over 1200% by the end of his last ten years as manager.

Why, then, do so many individual investors imagine they can do as well with a fraction of the effort? The answer often lies in the fact that those investors seldom set out to buy something, but—with the help of a talented broker—they somehow end up owning something! Besides being so much easier than doing their own homework, if the investment goes sour they can always blame the broker! On the other hand, if it does well, they can take full credit for being so clever.

This, of course, often leads the investor to believe that he possesses investment insight. So, when the next idea is presented, he greedily snaps it up. But now he will probably return those gains, so effortlessly achieved the first time, to the gods of the auction. Such an outcome often results in the now-humbled investor pulling out of the investment at the worst time—vowing never to return, and blaming everyone but himself.

Sound familiar? If it hasn't happened to you, it probably has to someone you know. First of all, most experts agree that you should have at least $50,000 to start a portfolio of individual stocks, have access to reliable information, and have the time and judgment to properly manage it. But, by definition, a small investor has only a fraction of the $50,000, little knowledge of what to do with what information is available, and then only a few hours a week to manage it.

One possible solution is to put together a portfolio of mutual funds, as discussed in the previous section, but then use whatever surplus may be available over the basic $5,000 to start a portfolio of stocks. Just make certain to use money that, if lost, will not painfully affect your present lifestyle.

Unlike most mutual funds which must buy hundreds of different issues to avoid disruptive concentrations, the individual investor can build a diversified stock portfolio with as few as six to ten issues. Here diversity does not depend on the number of stocks, but the variety. A portfolio with equal dollar amounts in six to ten unrelated stocks has only slightly more risk than one with hundreds of issues. Since the individual investor is hard-pressed to keep up with what's going on in more than a half-dozen companies at a time, this is good news. So whether your six-issue portfolio is worth $10,000 or $100,000, it will require the same effort to manage.

Unlike picking mutual funds, however, reducing the list of a bunch of stocks to a handful of winners won't be as easy or as cheap as studying a few magazine surveys. But, as demonstrated in the section on mutual funds, you can use the process of elimination to simplify things.

First, let's discuss then eliminate the following barriers to making a profit:

1) The Margin Account
2) Writing Covered Call Options
3) Selling Short
4) Initial Public Offerings (IPOs)
5) Penny Stocks

1) **The Margin Account** is an exciting device for applying leverage to your money. It allows you to buy twice as many shares of a stock as you could buy in a regular (cash) account for the same money. Here's how it works: You buy $10,000 worth of a stock by putting up $5,000 and borrowing another $5,000 from the broker who then charges you, the small investor, the highest legal rate of interest.

Now the stock has to appreciate at least one-half as fast as the interest rate you are being charged just to break even. If the stock hits a nasty dip instead, well there's this thing called a "margin call," which means: Send more money now! If you don't, there's another thing called a "sell-out," which means: We've sold your shares—sorry. It's not a pretty picture. Margin accounts are for the short-term trader, not the long-term investor.

2) **Writing Covered Call Options** is what happens when you sell (write) call options to someone who thinks the underlying stock is going to go up, which, if true, will make his options go up as well; but then you own the underlying stock which you hope will just hold its own. Because if your stock goes above the option "strike price," then it will be called away (assigned) at the option expiration date—when you may kiss any further appreciation goodbye.

Confused? Good! So why do people do it? Well, the idea is that the money (premium) you get when you write the call, when added to the dividend that the stock pays, will enhance your yield. Also, you're protected by the amount of the premium if the stock goes down. However, while covered call writing is the most conservative strategy involving stock options, the high commissions charged the small investor will usually offset any meaningful long-term benefits. As for buying options, just keep in mind that stock options, index options, and futures options are all "wasting assets"—barring a significant move in the underlying security, their value can reach zero upon their expiration date. For now, avoid options in all their forms.

3) **Selling Short** is what you do when you think the price of a stock is going down, but rather than avoid it altogether you sell it to someone who thinks it is going up. But since you are short the shares (you don't own them), you must first borrow them from the broker. If you can buy them back later for less than what you sold them for, you'll make money.

In the meantime, the credit you created in your "margin account" is not yours to spend. In fact, to do the transaction you first have to make a 50% cash deposit, and if the stock then goes up instead of down, you'll be charged interest on the appreciation. That's not all. You may have to come up with even more cash, and if that's impossible, the broker will "buy back" the stock and lock in a tidy loss in your account. It's automatic.

In short, selling short is not for you—besides, many consider the activity downright un-American.

4) When the stock of a company is first made available to the public, it's called an **Initial Public Offering** or IPO. It's regarded by many to be the most exciting way to

participate in the growth of corporate America—next to having their own thriving business. The prospect of being among the first shareholders of the next IBM, Xerox, or Microsoft is irresistible. The reality—sorry, more cold water: it is seldom profitable. Few IPOs have ever outperformed the S&P 500. Over the last ten years only one-third made any money for their investors. If you think researching a seasoned issue is difficult, try it when all you have is a "red herring" (preliminary prospectus).

One factor that will most likely save you from yourself is that if a new issue has been heavily promoted (hyped), you won't be able to get any shares anyway. They'll all go to the broker's biggest and best accounts. But take heart. If you still want to play after the dust has settled and the short-term traders have bailed out, those shares may be in ample supply and a lot cheaper then.

Finally, keep in mind that taking a company public is for many founders the first opportunity to convert their blood, sweat, and tears into serious cash. By including a large portion of their own shares in the offering, they stand to become instant millionaires; since the shares that cost them a penny, say, may soon go for fifteen dollars. Are you about to buy a company which may lose its reason for success—its founders—to a long fishing trip?

If you must play in the IPO market, at least try to buy shares from a prominent brokerage firm—one who is a member of the underwriting syndicate.

5) **Penny Stocks** - the path to quick and total losses is seldom shorter than the one leading to small so-called emerging growth stocks being hyped and sold by small emerging growth brokerage firms. The prices of the shares are never quoted in the newspaper. So the market is

whatever they say it is, and official company reports are
hard to get—if they even exist.

So hang up the phone and stick with the actively traded
stocks listed on the major exchanges or the
over-the-counter (OTC) markets.

Investing, like most aspects of life, seldom involves only
black or white situations. There may come a time when
one or more of the above devices—except penny stocks—is
appropriate for the small investor. But until you have
some relevant experience under your belt, leave them for
those who prefer the fast lane to watching the
horizon—their time horizon that is.

As discussed in the section on mutual funds, when
starting a portfolio of individual stocks, you should
consider your stage of life before establishing your
portfolio objective. Remember, the longer your time
horizon the more volatility you can justify, but also, the
more time you must spend keeping up with events within
the companies you're following.

An aggressive growth portfolio will concentrate on the
stocks of companies which are in the early stages of their
growth. They seldom pay a dividend but instead allocate
any profit to finance further corporate expansion. Their
stocks tend to be much more volatile than the "market."

A so-called growth/income portfolio contains the stocks
of more mature companies whose growth has leveled off,
but who now pay a generous dividend. It may also contain
utility stocks: the stocks of companies that provide
essential services such as electric power, natural gas, etc.
These types of stocks are likely to have average to low
volatility.

An income portfolio may consist of all utility stocks or
all bonds or a combination of both. While the volatility of

the bond market has increased in recent years, it has remained considerably lower than that of the stock market. Here you're looking for steady income and, as they say, "conservation of capital."

Barriers to profit and investment objectives aside, how do you pick the appropriate six to ten stocks that will make up your portfolio? Here we're at a fork in the road. Both paths will take you to your ultimate destination: a suitable stock selection. However, one path covers a winding, hilly, but scenic route; the other is like an interstate highway—faster but less interesting.

Let's look at the interstate first: Hundreds of companies are analyzed in the research reviews published by *The Value Line Investment Survey* and the *Standard & Poors (S&P) Stock Reports,* to name the two most prominent. Several hundred dollars each will get you a yearly subscription. Better yet, your large public library offers the use of both surveys, including current updates, for free. While both supply detailed reports, The Value Line also offers its trademarked shortcuts for ranking stocks as to their relative volatility (Safety) and expected price performance (Timeliness). It could be as easy as 1,2,3:

1) From the "current opinion" reports in those surveys, pick the six unrelated industries with the best prospects for slow but steady growth; altogether, there are about twenty-four industry groups to choose from. Some examples are: Aerospace, Consumer Products, Food, Health Care Service, Transportation, and Utilities.

2) From within the selected industries, pick six to ten stocks which are ranked by Value Line as follows: Number 1 for Timeliness, and between 1 and 3 for Safety.

3) Review subsequent reports weekly, at first, for updates about your stocks; be especially alert to changes in the ranking numbers.   This is not to suggest frequent trading within your portfolio, but to give you a sense of how various events may affect your holdings.

Although this "interstate highway" approach is easy, it has some drawbacks: First, by the time Value Line has decided to rank a stock Number 1 for Timeliness, chances are the market has already started to move it up. What's left is any price appreciation from there to its fair market value. So while you may be able to "buy low and sell high," you are unlikely to buy at the very bottom and sell at the top. But don't worry about it. Doing so consistently is all but impossible.

Second, this approach, if left here, precludes short-term trading strategies for both containing downside risk as well as taking advantage of unexpected but short-lived upturns in one or more of your stocks.   But even with these drawbacks, if you stick with a long time horizon, and buy and hold six to ten of the most timely unrelated stocks, chances are your portfolio would outpace inflation by a good margin even if you ignored it for five years.

Now for the "scenic route": Rankings for volatility and expected performance, while an important key to stock selection, is only the beginning of an **in-depth** process for building a portfolio. In fact, one approach is to search out stocks that are not even followed by analysts, much less ranked by them. These are often obscure, unglamorous, slow-growth companies.   The idea here is to find a company whose stock is priced well below its true (intrinsic) value, accumulate it slowly, before large institutions jump on the band wagon, and then wait.   It could take a few years, but the market eventually takes notice and rewards the early bird.

Easier said than done, however. Pick up a copy of the book *Security Analysis* by Graham and Dodd and you'll see what I mean. Assessing intrinsic value involves a highly technical process that could take the fun out of picking stocks, if not the accuracy.

An easier course would be to examine any investment newsletter which specializes in uncovering those "hidden gems." The *Hulbert Financial Digest* in Alexandria, Virginia (703 683-5905) covers such letters and ranks them as to the performance of their recommendations. A one-year subscription goes for $135, but introductory offers are often at half price. You might also find a copy at the library.

In addition, for forty-nine dollars (as of 1993) you can join the **American Association of Individual Investors** (AAII) in Chicago (312 280-0170). They are a non-profit association which accepts no advertising—sort of like *Consumer Reports* magazine. Included among the many features offered their membership is information on promising stocks with little or no following among securities analysts—so-called "shadow stocks."

The idea here is to buy stocks which are out of the lime-light because conventional wisdom has misperceived their true value. You can accumulate shares at your leisure. Then when the market finally takes notice, maybe three to five years later, you may be in a position to sell your shares to the late-comers now scrambling to buy at much higher prices.

While the premise of this book is that you can build a successful portfolio without the advice of a stockbroker, who has places to go and rich people to see, you will have to transact trades through some kind of brokerage firm. The question is will it be through a full-service firm or a discount house? The answer: it might be both. Why? Because some full-service firms also provide their customers with "special situation" reports which may include shadow stocks as well as stocks presently misperceived and thus "out of favor" in conventional terms. Using computer screens, their analysts uncover hidden assets of a company: maybe long-held real estate, on the books at original cost; or, maybe the sum total of the individual businesses making up the company is worth more than the market value of its stock.

Whatever, the profit opportunities can be significant, and the cost to you, the small investor, in slightly higher commissions—over discount rates—may be well worth it. On the other hand, those selections you make from your own research will most likely be bought through a discount broker. Just be aware that while many discount brokers grant up to a 70% discount from full-service rates to a high volume trader, you would probably qualify for less than a 20% discount on a typical 100 share transaction.

If you hear about a company whose stock is quoted in the newspaper but isn't mentioned in S&P, Value Line, or other surveys, then what you need to do next is really beyond the scope and mission of this book. But, briefly, you would look at the company as if the stock market didn't exist, and you could buy the whole company if you wanted to. First, telephone their Shareholder Relations department and ask for the most recent 10K and 10Q (annual and quarterly reports)—not to be confused with the glossy, picture-filled literature from Public Relations.

At the same time, request their latest proxy statement. Once received, you will need to analyze the financial and other data, including locating or calculating such things as the current ratio, price/earnings ratio, cash flow, and book value to name a few. Then, and here's the rub, you will have to be able to tell whether the numbers are good, bad, or indifferent. And that, dear reader, is found in another, very heavy, book.

Before spending too much time with the numbers, eliminate from further consideration those companies whose products you don't understand—too high-tech or whatever, or those you just don't like. Also avoid any company presently up against intense competition from other companies, and any whose stock is highly volatile.

If it's a local company, consider a personal visit to their corporate offices for a tour. But do your homework first so you can ask intelligent questions. Don't, however, expect lots of inside information because you won't get it. Here you're most interested in the look of the place and the attitudes of the people you meet there.

Obviously, there are no sure-fire ways to pick winning stocks whether taking the "interstate" or the "scenic route." However, the following are a couple of single-feature ideas which have been used with good results:

1) **High Yielding Blue Chips**—look through the *S&P Stock Guide*, a booklet also found at the library, and select the six stocks with the highest dividend yield from among the thirty stocks that make up the Dow Jones Industrial Average (DJIA). You'll find the "Dow thirty" listed in the "Money and Investing" section of *The Wall Street Journal*. Being blue-chip companies, they're not likely to go belly-up any time soon. Also, the higher yield (annual dividend/current price) often means that their stock prices are depressed, so you can collect a nice dividend while waiting for the price to move back up. Keep in mind

that over the long haul, one-half the total return on your portfolio can come from dividends.

2) **Price/Cash Flow Ratio**—The most popular indicators used to find bargain priced stocks have been the price/earnings ratio (P/E) and the price/book value ratio. Both, however, have problems: Earnings are, after all, whatever the company's accountants say they are. And book value (assets minus liabilities) doesn't adjust for inflation, so some company assets, like real estate, may be greatly undervalued. Cash flow, on the other hand, is pretax income with those expenses that the accountants love to play with, such as depreciation and amortization, added back in. However, finding a standard "market" cash flow number, as a basis for comparison, is difficult because the number will vary depending on the level of precision used to calculate it. For the sake of discussion, let's just say that an analyst calculates the market price/cash flow ratio to be approximately 15:1. Now, not to confuse things further, but, this and other ratios are most often stated as **multiples**. In this case, the analyst would say that the market is trading at 15 times cash flow. So, if you have uncovered a stock with a multiple 30% below that, say its price is 10 times cash flow, and its cash flow hasn't fluctuated greatly from year to year, then it's probably a good buy. Finally, remember *The Value Line Investment Survey* mentioned earlier? If Value Line has a report on the stock, the graph at the top of the page includes a "cash flow line." If the "monthly price ranges" are well below an up-sloping cash flow line, that suggests a bargain as well.

Whatever methods you use to select the stocks for your portfolio and before making a purchase, look up the "ex-dividend date" in the *S&P Stock Guide* on any of your choices which pay a dividend. The significance of the "ex date" is that shares purchased on or after that date will not pay the upcoming quarterly dividend. So if the ex date is only a couple weeks away, then delay purchase until afterwards. Otherwise you'll be paying the full price for the dividend, but only keeping what's left after your taxes. Better to buy after the ex date when the price usually drops by the amount of the dividend. This advice also applies when contemplating the purchase of a mutual fund. If, on the other hand, you *know* the stock is about to take a rocket ride to the moon, then waiting past the ex-dividend date may not be advisable. Then again, if that is going to be your approach to investing, you probably should be reading a "get-rich-quick" book found on the "best sellers" shelf of your bookstore.

If, in the process, you did not check the recent price history of your selections, this would be a good time to do so. No sense in buying if a stock is in the middle of a free-fall, or well into a sharp run-up in price. If that's the case, you should wait for the dust to settle, and then reexamine the situation. The stock may be too volatile for your program.

As the proud owner of **stocks**, your long range objective should be capital appreciation (growth). As the proud owner of **bonds**, however, your objective should be steady income. Not that you can't take a capital gain in a bond portfolio—remember that whenever interest rates drop, your bonds will increase in market value. And the further out the maturity date, the more the price will move for a given change in interest rates. It's just that if you do sell, you'll be hard-pressed to improve your income when you reinvest the proceeds in bonds of equal quality and maturity.

For example, say you own 10% bonds that cost you $10,000 (par); your annual income is $1,000. If the rate on new issues drops to 8.5%, your bonds will jump to say $11,000—a tempting 10% increase in market value. So you sell them and reinvest the proceeds in the new 8.5% bond. Your annual income is now 8.5% of $11,000 or $935—plus Uncle Sam is eagerly awaiting the taxes due on that $1,000 profit you took. Hmmmmm!?! Trading bonds seldom makes sense for the small investor, so plan to buy high quality issues and hold them to their maturity dates.

The task of deciding whether a bond issuer will be able to pay its creditors (investors) periodic interest and the principal at maturity is made easy thanks to bond rating services such as **Moody's** and **Standard & Poor's**. While, for instance, the **S&P** ratings run AAA, AA, A, BBB, etc., stick to the higher grade AAA, AA issues. The yield is a little lower, but you can sleep nights knowing it would take two or three downgrades (to say, CCC) before the notion of a default—failure to make the interest payments—began to loom on the horizon. Just keep in mind that AAA rated U.S. Treasury or Agency bonds are of higher quality, and will yield less, than AAA corporate bonds. At the same time, the quality of AAA rated municipal bonds is higher than corporates but lower than Treasuries—yet the yield is lower than both. Confused? It's because the interest paid on municipal bonds is tax-exempt so people in high tax brackets can benefit from owning them, and so the municipalities—the states, cities, school districts, and water districts can float bond issues at low rates.

But because of this tax-exempt thing, comparing Treasuries and corporates with "munis" is like comparing apples and oranges—until you determine what the yield would be on the munis if they were taxable. It's called the "taxable equivalent yield." Don't panic! A simple calculation produces the necessary figure for any tax rate (see Appendix E to see how). For example, in September 1993, yields on long-term bonds were as follows:

AAA U.S. Treasury bonds......... 6.00% - taxable
AAA corporate bonds.............. 6.79% - taxable
AAA/AA municipal bonds......... 5.00% - tax-exempt

The taxable equivalent yield of the munis then becomes:

5.88% for a 15% tax-bracket investor
6.94% for a 28% tax-bracket investor
7.25% for a 31% tax-bracket investor
7.81% for a 36% tax-bracket investor

As you can see, it makes no sense to buy munis if you're in the 15% bracket: Compared to Treasuries, you give up 0.12% of yield and sacrifice quality to boot. However, once you're in the 28% bracket, or higher, high-grade (AAA, AA) munis begin to make sense.

Whatever class of bond you choose for your program, the language is basically the same—baffling. For instance, when talking about stock prices, a "point" is worth $1.00; with bonds, a point is worth $10.00. Why the difference? Well, stock prices are quoted in dollars: A share of XYZ quoted at 18-1/8 equals $18.125. While bond prices are quoted as a percentage of par: ABC bonds quoted at 97 (called, would you believe, the dollar price) means 97% of $1,000 (usually) or $970. I say usually because unless the bond is a "Ginnie Mae" or some other mortgage-backed security, the face value and par are the same. So when a stock moves up 1/2 point, it's up 1/2 of $1.00 or 50 cents per share; when a bond dollar price moves up 1/2 point, it's up 1/2% of $1000.00 or $5.00 per bond. But that's not all!! Bonds are most frequently quoted on the basis of "yield to maturity" (say 7.10), but then you'll need a bond yield table or a small computer to find the dollar price. And guess what? When the yield of a bond changes, it changes in terms of "basis points!" It's true! Yet another kind of point to think about along with the terms "current yield" and "yield to the call." Finally, let's not forget that when yields go up, the dollar price goes down, and vice-versa.

For those who care, the following example of "bondspeak" along with a translation might help matters a bit:

"I just bought 65 of the Treasury 9-1/2s of 18. I paid 95 for a ten oh two (10.02). I picked up 20 basis points."

> Translation: 65 = $65,000 face amount—par (due at maturity)
>
> Treasury = U.S. Treasury bonds
>
> 9-1/2s = 9.5% coupon (fixed rate of interest)
>
> 18 = the year 2018 (when bonds mature)
>
> 95 = 95% of 65,000 or 61,750 (dollar price)
>
> 10.02 = yield to maturity
>
> 20 basis pts = 0.20% more yield than previous holding

Happily, there is a way to avoid all the confusion: Buy bonds out of new issues—the so-called primary market. Here, all buyers pay the same price. Whereas, in the secondary—used bond—market, the small investor pays the highest dealer markup, and he or she has little information to compare yields with. Most new bonds are priced at par or $1,000 per bond—which means that a U.S. Treasury note issued at par with an 8.40 coupon will have a yield to maturity of 8.40% and a current yield of 8.40%. No table or computer needed here.

To further complicate matters, many corporate and municipal bonds have "call features" which allow the issuer, in times of falling interest rates, to redeem (pay off) the bonds many years before the maturity date. While you may receive a premium, say 103% of par, for bonds that cost you par, you will be forced to reinvest your proceeds at those lower rates. This does not make for happy campers. So choose bonds that are either noncallable altogether, or for at least ten years. Incidently, the U.S. Treasury no longer issues callable bonds.

As with building a stock portfolio, a bond portfolio should be structured with long term objectives in mind. While the difference in yield—the spread—between short-term and long-term bonds varies with economic conditions, the usual pattern is for long-term bonds to have the higher yield. Therefore, the temptation, for the beginner, is to buy only long term bonds. The risk here is that if rates go up further, at a time when you need some cash, you'll be forced to sell at a loss.

A simple and more sensible approach is to organize the portfolio so that an equal number of bonds mature in five, ten, fifteen, and twenty years. That way, after five years, all maturities have shifted forward, and the "five year" bond pays off. You could then reinvest the proceeds in the space now available for twenty year (higher yielding) bonds—and so forth.

There is of course no guarantee that, over the years, this method will achieve maximum yields, but the results are likely to exceed those of a portfolio built around some expert's interest rate forecast, and do so with a lot less trouble.   In addition, you are creating a window of opportunity to pick up higher yields every five years.   In the meantime, the bond market can fluctuate all it wants because you're holding everything until maturity anyway. If later events require you to sell part of the portfolio for needed cash, you can take it from the short end where the bonds will be trading close to par.

Of course, the same technique can be used for investing in the cash equivalent (liquid) portion of your portfolio.   In this case, however, space your CDs, Treasury bills or notes to mature every three to six months.   This way your window of opportunity for higher yields will appear every three to six months.

As an informed small investor, you will probably open an account with a discount broker unless you plan to use the research reports which a full-service broker can provide.   However, it is possible to by-pass the broker altogether when purchasing U.S. Treasury securities such as bills, notes, and bonds.   To do so, call the nearest Federal Reserve Bank—your commercial bank should have the number—and ask that "Treasury Direct" forms and brochures be mailed to you.   Armed with this information, you can buy new Treasury issues at the auction, and pay the same price as the million bond buyer.

While the variety of bonds and bond-like investments is almost endless, there is one other type worth mentioning here: the zero coupon bond.   Created by the ever-enterprising brokerage industry, the "zero" is either a coupon that has been stripped off the original U.S. Treasury, corporate, or municipal bond, or is the stripped principal itself.   It is then repackaged as a bond that pays no periodic interest, and is priced at a deep discount from its face value—like a U.S. Savings bond. Upon maturity, the full face value is paid out. They don't make sense for an "income" portfolio, but they do when you plan to fund a specific goal. For instance, $10,000 worth of U.S. Treasury STRIPS due in 20 years would cost you about $3,000 today.

At the same time, $10,000 worth of coupon bonds would cost you $10,000 for a current issue, and the small semiannual coupon payments of, say, $295 would be difficult to reinvest in any meaningful way. With zeros, however, reinvestment is automatic.

Because they tend to be more volatile than coupon bonds, zeros should be held to maturity. In the meantime, Uncle Sam will insist that you pay annual taxes on the interest accrued—but not paid—so put them in a tax-deferred retirement plan such as a Keogh or IRA account. The exception to this rule would be a special class of zero coupon corporate bond where the accrued interest accumulates tax-deferred. They are called "Deferred Interest Securities" or DINTS for short. Be careful though—they often carry low credit ratings. Municipal zeros are of course tax-exempt, but they are hard to find and difficult to comparison shop as they aren't listed anywhere.

Speaking of comparison shopping: since zeros are a brokerage product, you will be paying a dealer markup wherever you go. So you'll need to do a little homework before calling your broker for a quote. First, get familiar with where and how zeros are listed in the newspaper. In *The Wall Street Journal*, corporate zeros can be found under "New York Exchange Bonds." For example the Allied Corp. zeros due August 1, 1999 are shown as AlldC zr99. Under "close" the price is, say, 48-3/8. If you could buy it there, $483.75 would become $1,000 on August 1, 1999. The most easily traded zeros—U.S. Treasury STRIPS—are found under "Treasury Bonds, Notes & Bills." Also offered by dealers are Treasury zeros with such acronyms as CATS, TIGRs, and LIONS. They are not as liquid as the STRIPS, nor are you likely to find a printed quote on them.

Next, decide what maturity year will fit your game plan. Then call your broker and say, for example:

> "I need a competitive offer of Treasury STRIPS due in 2011, the most actively traded issue, dollar price, and yield to maturity. I have about $5,000 to invest."

By saying "competitive" you are suggesting that you will be looking at other offers. Brokers don't like it, but it will help you get a fair price. Remember, as a small investor, you will pay a higher price for a lower yield—the markup could be over five percent of the initial dollars invested. In other words, the million-bond buyer might see an offer of 18 to yield 8.85% for the STRIPS of 2011—where you might see 19 to yield 8.55%. Say the broker returns with an offer of 19. Then say: "What is the face amount?" If he says $26,000, your cost should be $4,940 or 19% of $26,000; if he says $27,000, your cost should be $5,130 (see Appendix F for more details). Check the newspaper to see if he is in the ballpark, but keep in mind that prices on actively traded issues change frequently.

So, now that you have some ideas about how to pick your own stocks and bonds, what's next? Well, if you don't already have a broker or you don't know a happy customer of one, then now is the time to make a few phone calls. Try a few well-known firms—discount (see Appendix I), full-service, or both—and ask for application forms to open a "cash account" and a copy of their money market fund prospectus. If you call full-service firms, also ask for a copy of their latest list of recommendations.

Since you're not looking to the broker for specific investment advice, select the firm which is most responsive to your requests for information. Later, they will also be responsive to your orders. Next, complete the forms and send them back with a check for your initial investment along with a note instructing them to buy money market funds. This way your investment capital is both earning interest and available to pay for your trades on the settlement date (usually five working days after the trade date). Also, be sure to note on the account forms that your purchases are to be held by the broker in "street name" for your account. You do this because there are few cases where taking delivery of the actual stock and bond certificates makes any sense—lost or stolen certificates are expensive and time consuming to replace not to mention impossible to sell.

When you're ready to start buying stocks, keep the transactions simple. Buy one company's stock at a time and then only after your research suggests excellent long term growth prospects. Try to buy equal dollar amounts of each stock for a balanced portfolio, and do so in 100 share lots to avoid "odd lot" charges. The call to your broker might go like this:

> "Hi, this is Phil Hill, Account # 427-1234. I'd like to buy some Puddle Jumper Air, symbol PDL. Where is it trading now? That's 18-1/2? OK, buy 100 shares 'at the market.'"

When you say: "at the market," you are telling the broker that you want to own the stock at whatever price it's trading at when your order is executed.   In the above example, unless your stock is caught in the middle of a trading frenzy, you might pay between 18-3/8 and 18-5/8 per share. An often used but not recommended alternative is to give the broker a "limit" order to buy the shares at, say, 18-1/4. The belief (hope) is that the stock will drop there briefly. What usually happens is instead of going down the price heads up, and you, now a speculator, end up changing your "limit" to 18-3/4 before you can buy it.

The lesson here is: buy and sell stock "at the market." There are few reasons for the small investor to do otherwise. After placing a market order, your broker should either confirm the trade then and there, or call you back shortly. If PDL continued to trade at 18-1/2, your 100 shares would cost $1,850—plus the commission.

Speaking of commissions: they are not always spelled out on the confirmation ticket your broker sends you, after each trade. It depends on the market the security is traded on. For example:

1) When buying "listed" stocks (those traded on the **New York Stock Exchange**, the **American Stock Exchange, etc.**), you will be quoted the "ask" price. When selling, you will be quoted the "bid" price. Your confirmation will show the price, as executed, and the commission—separately.

2) When buying "Over-the-Counter" (OTC) stocks, you will be quoted the **sum** of the "offering" price and some mark up. When selling you will be quoted the **difference** of the "bid" price and some mark down. Therefore, the confirmation of a purchase will show only

the quoted price (offer + mark up). For a sale: the quoted price (bid - mark down). The commission is not shown.

3) Listed corporate bonds and some Treasuries are traded in small denominations on the **New York Bond Exchange**, where commissions are not included in the quoted price, but are shown on the confirmations. But, since bonds are generally quoted on a yield-to-maturity basis, tacking on a commission after quoting a price makes the yield number look better than it is. However, since most corporates, Treasuries, and all municipals are traded over-the-counter where commissions are not spelled out, the yield figure is accurate—it's just that your cost to do the trade is unknown.

In theory, your broker buys the bonds on the bid side from another dealer, and sells them to you on the offering side—the commission being in the "spread." The problem is, unlike the listed markets, over-the-counter quotes can vary between dealers. So it's important to be in touch with the average yields for bonds you may be looking at. How close theory is to reality will depend on the size of the order, the direction of the market, and sometimes, how closely the dealer thinks his customer is in touch with the market.

While you should design your portfolio for the long term, it's unlikely that you would put it aside and ignore it for months at a time. Those are your hard-earned bucks, after all. So stay abreast of what's happening in the six to ten stocks in your portfolio. If unexpected news causes a large price move in one of your positions, consider your next move carefully. If the stock falls sharply, wait for the dust to settle before selling. Chances are it will bounce up some even if the news is really bad. If the drop was just an overreaction and all the reasons you bought are still intact, then buy some more shares if you can.

If, on the other hand, the price went up, say, twenty percent within a few weeks for no apparent reason, then consider selling half your position. Then if the stock settles back down to its "trend line"—very likely—you could then buy back even more shares with the proceeds. In the meantime, the other half of your original position is available just in case the stock continues its sharp uncharacteristic upturn. Don't be too hasty here either: remember, you'll be paying commissions when you sell, and when you buy back, as well as paying taxes on the profit.

One final strategy: If you're going to be out of touch with things for a while, then consider putting "stops" around your positions. Say you own 200 XYZ at an average cost of $20 per share. Tell your broker to:

"Sell 200 XYZ at 15, stop loss, good 'till cancelled."

If the stock falls to 15, your order becomes a "market" order and will be executed at or around 15. Taking a 25% loss isn't much fun, especially if the stock goes back up before you get home, but it is a way of limiting your losses if the stock suddenly becomes a dog.

The other half of the strategy might be to say:

"Sell 100 XYZ at 25, good 'till cancelled."

If the stock spikes up 25% and trades at 25 or better, you'll be out with a profit on half your position—as in the example above.

There are of course many more possible hedging strategies; the library is full of imposing textbooks about investing in stocks and bonds. And while your program should focus on building net worth rather than on short-term, taxable trading profits, bear in mind that things change. Of the thirty blue chip stocks making up the Dow Jones Industrial Average fifteen years ago, fourteen have been replaced. So keep track of your six to ten holdings, and make changes when it's warranted, but when you are within two or three years of your time horizon, move into money market funds, CDs, and T-bills. Your retirement plan or your grandchild will be glad you did.

Hard Cash

NOTES

IV

IRA ACCOUNTS AND OTHER TAX DEFERRALS

While the average American family saves between four and five percent of its income for such things as retirement, rainy days, and so forth, the savings rate among Japanese workers is over sixteen percent. Why the Japanese save so much more can best be explained within the context of their unique culture, but the fact that they pay only a one percent capital gains tax may have a little something to do with their relatively recent shift away from postal savings accounts to growth stocks.

Since our friends in Congress devised the peculiar income tax structure that punishes the investor and rewards the debtor, perhaps the retirement plans they created over the last couple decades was an attempt at self redemption. Before looking at those and other plans, however, let me clarify some terms: **Tax-deductible** means that you subtract that amount from your income before figuring your taxes; **tax-deferred** means that any increases in the value of your investments are taxed only after you start to withdraw the money. Now, the following is a list of tax-deferred investments created by either Wall Street, the U.S. Congress, or the insurance industry:

A **401(k) PLAN**, if offered by your company, should be funded to the maximum allowed first, before considering other plans. That's because many companies fully match your pretax contributions up to 3% of your salary, and partially match up to 6%. In those cases, the 401(k) plan provides a tremendous tax-deferred growth opportunity even if the investment vehicles available to the plan turn out to be only mediocre performers. The minimum yearly investment is 1% of your salary; the maximum is 10% or $8,994, whichever is less. Why $8,994? That's the limit for 1993—future limits are adjusted to the inflation rate. There are no fees, but it's difficult to withdraw any money before age 59-1/2. If you do, you pay income taxes on the amount withdrawn plus you're subject to a 10% surcharge. However, you are allowed to borrow limited amounts from the plan, and pay yourself the interest on the loan.

The **IRA ACCOUNT**, up until the Tax Reform Act of 1986, provided the means for all employees to make a tax-deductible contribution of up to $2,000 of their earnings to a tax-deferred retirement plan. However, starting with only $2,000 made buying individual securities difficult, unless you bought zero coupon bonds. As a result, the IRA account became a natural for parking all types of mutual funds. Accordingly, billions of dollars poured into mutual fund IRAs over the decade to follow. Then, just when the years of compounded, tax-deferred returns emerged before the masses, tax reform took away full deductibility from everyone except those least able to put up the $2,000 and those not covered by a company pension plan.

So what's a mother to do? Well, if you have any investment dollars available after fully funding a 401(k) or other employer-matching program, and you're single, making $25,000 or less, or married and jointly making $40,000 or less, then fund an IRA account. Your contribution would be fully tax-deductible. If, on the other hand, you make more than those amounts, and you're in a company pension plan, then your contribution would be partially deductible or not deductible at all (peruse the IRA literature for the current details). This being the case, and you plan to invest your after tax dollars in a stock mutual fund IRA, then at least the earnings will be tax-deferred.

However, if a more conservative Treasury/corporate bond mutual fund is on your mind, then it may make more sense to just buy a municipal bond fund outside of the IRA. Why? I'll explain in the paragraph on municipal bonds to follow. So, if you are *not* covered by a company pension, then your IRA contribution is fully deductible regardless of income. While there is no legal minimum investment, most mutual funds require at least $250 to get started. The maximum is $2,000 a year. As in other tax-deferred plans, if you withdraw money before age 59-1/2, you will pay taxes on that amount and be subject to a 10% surcharge as well. Administrative fees are $10 to $15 a year.

The **KEOGH** and **SEP-IRA** plans are designed for the self-employed individual. However, an employee who participates in a company retirement plan, a 401(k) plan, and an IRA account, may also open a Keogh and/or a SEP-IRA account, if he has a business on the side. A "Simplified Employee Pension-Individual Retirement Account" or SEP-IRA, for short, is easier to start and administer than a Keogh account, but is best suited to someone who works alone. That's because if you hire part-time workers, you may have to set up accounts for them also. In that case, the more complicated Keogh plan would be better because you need only make contributions for full-time workers. However, some Keoghs require an annual contribution, so you should have a stable business.

Thanks to the Omnibus Budget Reconciliation Act of 1993, starting January 1, 1994, the maximum annual tax-deductible contribution (indexed for inflation) to a typical Profit Sharing Plan is $22,500—down from $30,000—with a limit of 15% of earned income for the SEP-IRA and 25%

for the Keogh. No percentage or dollar limitation applies to a Defined Benefit Keogh. The same rules apply for early withdrawal as in other tax-deferred plans, and the annual administrative fees average about $30.

A **DEFERRED ANNUITY** contract is what you might consider for a long-range retirement plan if you have any money left over after funding a 401(k) plan, an IRA, and, if self-employed, a Keogh or SEP-IRA plan. Created by the insurance industry, annuities offer a tax-deferred return on two basic types of contracts: fixed and variable. A **fixed annuity** provides steady growth from preset interest rates. However, these rates may only be fixed for a few years before being subject to periodic adjustments. A **variable annuity** allows the policyholder to speculate on the stock or bond funds offered in the contract—funds which, incidently, may have no track record to speak of. The ultimate payout will depend strictly on the performance of those funds. While the policy accumulates earnings on a tax-deferred basis, the initial premium, whether deposited in a single payment or in installments, is *not* tax-deductible.

So once again, tax-exempt municipal bonds may be the better choice here. The minimum investment ranges between $5,000 and $10,000, but there is no maximum investment. This makes it a very attractive tax-deferred investment for the individual who can afford to fund it generously. Later, at retirement, you may take either a lump sum payment or receive monthly payments for life. If you opted for monthly payments, the insurance company, with the help of mortality tables, is betting that you won't outlive the available money.

Finally, early withdrawal also results in tax penalties: a 10% surcharge on top of ordinary income taxes. Add to that "surrender charges" between 5% and 10% of the accumulation value (the earnings over your initial premium) if you decide to get out in the first year, declining to 0% after 6 to 10 years. If you stay in for the duration, administrative fees run between $25 and $30 a year, in addition to the annual "mortality" and money management charges of between 2% and 3% of the total value of the portfolio.

In other words, their performance has to be really good to overcome all those fees and still make any sense. If, however, you're convinced an annuity contract fits your situation, just consider a couple of things: First, the insurance company offering the contract should be rated A+ by **A.M. Best**, for the past 15 years. Recent years have seen the ratings of a number of insurance companies drop because of their investment in the junk-bond market. Next, comparison shopping in the annuity marketplace is difficult because contracts differ widely from one product to another. If you just gotta have one, then check the library for recent back-issues of *Consumer Reports* magazine for help. They have written extensively on the subject.

GROWTH STOCKS can be the purest form of tax-deferred investing. Unless they pay a dividend, there is no tax consequence to owning them until you start to sell them—perhaps at retirement. At that point, you may even be in a lower tax bracket. Also, you can write-off any losses along the way—something you can't do when shares are held in a tax-deferred retirement plan. Finally, there are no legal minimum or maximum investment requirements, no annual fees, and no early withdrawal penalties.

Since the income from **MUNICIPAL BONDS** is not just tax-deferred but completely tax-exempt, they make more sense than an IRA portfolio of corporate or Treasury bonds, if you *cannot* take the $2,000 deduction for your IRA contribution and you're in, at least, the 28% tax bracket. That's because when you start to withdraw money from a non-deductible IRA, you will still owe taxes on the earnings portion, just not the yearly contributions. And since the taxable equivalent yield of munis is higher than, say, comparable Treasuries for a 28% bracket taxpayer, the long term results with munis are likely to be at least as good—probably better.

Although munis have no legal restrictions on investment size, no annual fees, and no withdrawal penalties, the smallest denomination available is $5,000, and you will pay a sales commission. Of course, a no-load tax-exempt bond mutual fund can be acquired with much less money. Finally, when you make a contribution to a non-deductible IRA account, you have to file an additional tax form (8606), and hang on to all the other related records forever, or until Congress changes the laws again—whichever comes first. If, on the other hand, you plan to build your IRA with potentially higher performing stocks or stock mutual funds, then even a non-deductible IRA would be appropriate.

As of this writing, there are several movements afoot within the halls of Congress to change the rules regarding IRA accounts in terms of tax-deductibility of contributions as well as withdrawal penalties. The investment opportunities and the rules surrounding them are subject to change. Just remember, there is no worthwhile investment opportunity that can't wait a few days or even weeks until you have looked into it and decided that it makes sense considering your circumstances.

V

LIMITED PARTNERSHIPS, COMPUTERS
& COCKTAIL PARTIES

In the mid 1970s, Wall Street bid a fond farewell to fixed-rate commissions. From that time forward they were required to negotiate [lower] rates with their most favored customers—the very active institutional investors. In no time at all, vigorous competition for business among the brokerage firms resulted in drastic reductions in commission revenues. This was followed shortly thereafter by a number of mergers as well as many old-line firms going out of business. Survival then depended on finding other sources of commission dollars.

The individual investor, then in tax brackets as high as 70%, suddenly zoomed into the foreground as Wall Street contemplated the limited partnership tax shelter. Soon, even investors of modest means were being offered units of limited partnership for as little as $5,000 each. The most popular were in such exciting ventures as oil and gas exploration, real estate, research & development, and feature motion pictures. All offered significant rates of return for the near future as well as tax write-offs sufficient to at least offset the initial investment—with some real estate deals offering write-offs between two and four times the cost of the unit.

Now, it was one thing to bet that some folks would not find oil deep in the ground, or make a few hit movies, or even find a cure for cancer, but quite another to bet that a piece of land with an office building or apartment house

wouldn't make money. After all, there's only so much
land, and real estate has always gone up—right?

Indeed, with inflation in the double digits, real estate
became a commodity with no downside in sight. But, as
thousands of small investors in limited partnerships later
learned, their general partners—the guys who actually ran
the business—had engaged in bidding contests, paying far
more than the property would ever be worth within the life
of the partnership. That eliminated any chance for a profit
upon the sale of the building. And matters were made
worse in over-built areas since sparsely occupied buildings
don't generate much cash flow.

The final blow was dealt many of these transactions
when the Tax Reform Act of 1986 was passed, thus
eliminating any write-offs yet to be taken—much to the
surprise of the investors who had been assured that their
tax benefits would be "grandfathered" (exempt from any
changes in the tax code). Down but not out, with
management fees running well below projections, some
promoters then devised a way to take out yet another level
of fees by merging several partnerships into a single
publicly traded company—it's called a "roll-up." They say
it's good for the shareholders because it spreads out the
risk, reduces administrative costs, and provides greater
liquidity (it's much easier to sell stock than partnership
units). What roll-ups have not done, however, is go up in
price, thanks to a sick real estate market. Whether a
recovery will ever allow the original investors to come out
whole is yet to be known.

After hearing from a number of investor groups,
Congress and the Securities and Exchange Commission
(SEC) became concerned that many original limited
partners had been pressured into voting for roll-ups, and

have moved to protect investors as future roll-ups are submitted for clearance.

Why am I telling you all this? Because anyone with a good imagination, the ability to borrow money for his small equity contribution, and the talent for raising lots of other people's money can become the general partner in an exciting, but totally unproven new business. Predictably, of all the publicly registered limited partnerships offered over the past ten or fifteen years, only a handful, which had any substance to them in the first place, ever achieved their original projections. And only a few of those outperformed a decent equity (stock) mutual fund over the same period. It was only the recent settlement of a multi-hundred-million dollar class-action lawsuit against a major Wall Street firm that enabled thousands of its limited-partnership investors to get back any of their original investment. And this only because the court decided the deals had been misrepresented to unsophisticated prospects.

Now for computers: Yes, it is possible to buy a personal computer with lightening-like processing speed and enormous memory capacity for under two thousand dollars. Thirty years ago a computer with less speed and memory cost millions, and filled a large room. But, there is also an almost infinite variety of investment software to choose from. The **American Association of Individual Investors** (mentioned earlier) offers a directory that should help to boil down the list. Just be careful that all the costs associated with the hardware, software, and hookups to wire services don't cut heavily into your profits. You probably need at least a $50,000 portfolio to really justify computer-aided-investing.

As for cocktail parties: These are the places you go to hear people brag about how they tripled their money in three weeks playing the stock, bond, or commodities markets, and to ask those same individuals what their portfolio has returned over the last five or ten years. Be prepared, in the latter case, for a few awkward moments of silence.

On the other hand, if you choose such parties to brag about how you have averaged 18% a year for the last ten years in a small collection of mutual funds, then don't be hurt when your listeners' responses include glazed-over eyes and stifled yawns. Let's face it: " Getting rich quick" is just more exciting, and suggests that those lucky few who do may have the "Midas touch." The problem is just that the ones who do it, in any given year, probably equal approximately the number of people struck by lightening over the same time. And only a few—investors, not lightening strike victims—ever repeat the performance.

So what's ahead for the rest of the nineties? Who knows. Many will forecast events to come; most will be wrong. So just stick with the basics: establish your "stage of life," pick the appropriate pie chart, choose the most promising and suitable mutual funds, stocks, or bonds, try to invest the same amount of money each month, and then give it all a chance to work.

Good luck!

APPENDIX A

Mutual Fund Formulas

If the net-asset-value (NAV) of a no-load fund is $17.23, then $1500 buys 87.057 shares (1500 / 17.23 = 87.057).

If a load fund has a sales charge of 5.5% and the NAV is $17.23, then the Offering Price (what you pay)
$$= NAV / (1 - Load)$$
$$= 17.23 / (1 - 0.055)$$
$$= 17.23 / 0.945$$
$$= 18.23$$
and $1500 buys 82.282 shares (1500 / 18.23 = 82.282).

Also, NAV = Offering Price x (1 - Load)
$$= 18.23 \text{ x } (1 - 0.055)$$
$$= 18.23 \text{ x } 0.945$$
$$= 17.23$$

And, Load = 1 - (NAV / Offering Price)
$$= 1 - (17.23 / 18.23)$$
$$= 1 - 0.945$$
$$= 0.055 = 5.5\%$$

APPENDIX B

Dollar Cost Averaging

Dollar-cost-averaging means to invest the same amount of money each period (monthly, quarterly, etc.) regardless of the apparent direction of the market. Let's compare an example of that with a one-time purchase:

I. Dollar Cost Averaging

Amount Invested	Month	Fund Price/ Share	Shares Purchased
$ 500	Jan	$15.237	32.815
$ 500	Apr	$12.429	40.228
$ 500	Jul	$15.382	32.506
$ 500	Oct	$17.193	29.082
$2000			134.631

The average cost per share is $14.855, ($2000 / 134.631).
October portfolio value is 2314.71 (17.193 x 134.631).

II. One-time purchase

Amount Invested	Month	Fund Price / Share	Shares Purchased
$2000	Jan	$15.237	131.259

The cost per share is $15.237.
October portfolio value is $2256.74 (17.193 x 131.259).

Over a period of upward-trending, but fluctuating market prices, dollar-cost-averaging will lower the average cost per share, when compared to infrequent lump-sum purchases. That, of course, means you end up with more shares—which is good.

APPENDIX C

Portfolio Performance Calculations

Calculating investment performance would be easy if you started with, say, $10,000, made no additions or withdrawals of cash, reinvested the dividends, and five years later had a portfolio worth $20,000. Your trusty pocket calculator would reveal a 14.87% compounded annual return, and you'd be pretty happy, especially if inflation had averaged 4% a year over the same period. But in the real world, you'll want to take a look at least once a quarter, and if you've been adding or withdrawing money along the way, you can *approximate* performance as in the following examples:

I.   Starting investment.........................$10000
     During 1st quarter you **added**...........$ 500
     End of quarter market value is, say.....$11150

     1) $500 / 2 = $250

     2) $10000 $11150
         + 250   - 250
         $10250 $10900

     3) $10900
         -10250
         $ 650

     4) 650 / 10250 = 0.063 = 6.3% return for 1st quarter

Continued on following page >

II.   Starting 2nd quarter at.......................$11150
       During 2nd quarter you **withdrew**..........$ 300
       End of quarter market value is, say........$11375

       1) $300 / 2 = $150

       2) $11150 $11375
              - 150   + 150
           $11000 $11525

       3) $11525
           -11000
           $ 525

       4) 525 / 11000 = 0.048 = 4.8% return for 2nd quarter

After the first quarter you may want to **annualize** the performance. That is, **if your portfolio keeps growing at 6.3% per
quarter** for the next three quarters, then what will the annual
return be? Well you could just say 6.3% x 4 = 25.2%, but that
would ignore the effects of compounding. So:

       From the basic formula for compounding, add 1 to
       0.063 = 1.063. Then calculate 1.063 x 1.063 x 1.063
       x 1.063 = 1.277. Now subtract 1 from 1.277 = 0.277
       = 27.7% annualized return.

If you've calculated the actual performance for each quarter, as
above, then you can calculate the annual return as follows.
Say qtr 1 = +6.3%; qtr 2 = +4.8%; qtr 3 = -2.4%; qtr 4 =
+5.1%; then:

Continued on following page >

1) Convert these returns back to decimals:
   +0.063; +0.048; -0.024; +0.051

2) Add 1 to each figure:
   +1.063; +1.048; +0.976; +1.051

3) Multiply together:
   1.063 x 1.048 x 0.976 x 1.051 = 1.143

4) Subtract 1 from 1.143 = 0.143 = 14.3% annual return.

APPENDIX D

Financial Statement Formulas

1) Acid Test Ratio (can they pay their bills)
   = (Current Assets - Inventory) / Current Liabilities

2) Book Value = Net Worth - Intangibles - Preferred Par*

3) Cash Flow (simple) = Net Income + Depreciation*

4) Current Ratio = Currents Assets / Current Liabilities

5) Dividend Yield = Annual Dividend per share / Market Price
   per share

6) Earnings = Net Income - Preferred Dividends*

7) Net Worth = Assets - Liabilities*

8) Price-Book Value Ratio = Market Price per share / Book
   Value per share

9) Price-Cash Flow Ratio = Market Price per share / Cash
   Flow per share

10) Price-Earnings Ratio (P/E) = Market Price per share /
    Earnings per share

11) Working Capital = Current Assets - Current Liabilities

***For per share figure, divide by number of common shares
outstanding.**

APPENDIX E

Taxable Equivalent Yield Calculation

In order to compare the yields between a taxable bond and a tax exempt municipal bond, it is necessary to determine what the yield of the "muni" would be if it were taxable. So, if the yield-to-maturity of a muni is, say, 7.10%, and your marginal tax bracket is 28%, then:

Taxable Equivalent Yield = Muni Yield / (1 - Tax Bracket)
$$= 7.10 / (1 - 0.28)$$
$$= 7.10 / 0.72$$
$$= 9.86$$

How does that yield compare with a taxable bond of comparable quality and maturity?

APPENDIX F

Zero Coupon Bond Calculations

Like U.S. Savings Bonds, "zeros" are purchased at a discount from par (the face amount—what you get when the bond matures). Unlike savings bonds, however, par is any multiple of $1,000 (1,000; 6,000; 83,000; etc.). Since zeros are quoted in terms of their yield-to-maturity and dollar price (some % of par), it would be helpful to know what par **should be** when offered the bonds by your broker. Let's say, for example, that you require a U.S. Treasury STRIP due in 20 years, and you have $10,000 to invest. The broker quotes you a dollar price of 17:25. Do the following calculations:

1) 17:25 = 17 & 25/32 = 17.78125% = 0.1778125
2) **Approximate** par = Dollars Invested / Dollar Price
            = $10,000 / 0.1778125 = $56,239.016

But, par must be to the nearest $1,000. So round down to $56,000. Then your cost to buy $56,000 worth of zeros = $56,000 x 0.1778125 = $9,957.50.

APPENDIX G

More About Bonds

Debt instruments run the gamut from commercial paper, certificates of deposit (CDs), bankers acceptances, U.S. Treasury securities, municipal and corporate bonds, and countless other variations on the theme. Because many such instruments are issued in large denominations, most individuals would be limited to the following:

TYPE	MINIMUM INVESTMENT	MATURITY WHEN ISSUED
Bank Certificates of Deposit (CDs)	$ 500	30 days to 5 years
Money Market mutual funds	$ 1,000	Daily (reinvested)
U. S. Treasury Bills	$10,000	3 months to 1 year
U. S. Treasury Notes	$ 5,000	2 years to 10 years
U. S. Treasury Bonds	$ 1,000	30 years
Corporate Bonds	$ 5,000	5 years to 20 years
Municipal Bonds	$ 5,000	1 year to 20 years

NOTE: You may, of course, find bonds with maturities all in between by looking in the secondary (used bond) market.

Price fluctuations for a given change in interest rates will vary greatly depending on the maturity of the bond. For instance, a bond with a 7% coupon purchased at par (to yield 7%) would fluctuate as shown in the table on the following page.

EXAMPLES OF BOND PRICE FLUCTUATIONS

TIME TO MATURITY	CHANGE IN INTEREST FROM 7% TO 8%	CHANGE IN INTEREST FROM 7% TO 5%
1 Year	- 1.00%	+ 1.00%
5 Years	- 4.00%	+ 8.75%
10 Years	- 6.75%	+ 15.50%
20 Years	- 10.00%	+25.13%

**Note: Beyond about 25 years bond prices tend to fluctuate equally
for a given change in interest rates.**

As mentioned earlier, it's important to stage bond investments so
that an equal number of bonds mature in, say, five, ten, fifteen
and twenty years. This "ladder" structure will eliminate the
temptation to trade bonds, and will create a window for
acquiring potentially higher yields in the longest maturities as the
shortest maturities come due. If raising cash becomes necessary,
the short term positions can be sold at little or no loss.

APPENDIX H

No-Load/Low-Load Mutual Funds
(Minimum initial investment $3,000 or less)

Following is a list of no-load or low-load mutual funds which, according to the 1993 *Business Week*-**Mutual Fund Scoreboard**, would make it through the screen shown on page 13. On a **risk-adjusted** basis, the stock funds have performed as well as, or better than the S&P 500 over the past five years (1988-1993). While the included stock funds have at least a ten-year track record, the bond funds have no less than a five-year track record of above average performance when measured against various bond indexes.

Higher than average volatility (risk) kept most maximum growth funds from passing through the screen, but such funds should make up about thirty-five percent of an "early career" portfolio. Just be sure to check turnover (trading activity), because two funds may generate the same impressive total return, but the one with the lower turnover will produce the higher **after-tax** return. For example, **Fund A** may actively trade the portfolio, taking many short-term taxable profits which may then be reinvested in additional shares of the fund.

Whether reinvested or not, short-term gains are taxed as ordinary income for the year taken. On the other hand, **Fund B** may hold some positions for much longer periods during which the stocks in the portfolio may appreciate substantially in value—so-called "paper profits." Of course, this growth remains untaxed until realized—when the stocks are sold. Such gains may then be taxed at the lower (long-term capital gains) rate.

Get the picture? Lower turnover = fewer taxable events and lower rates when they happen. If, however, the funds are held in a tax-deferred retirement account (IRA, 401(k), etc.), then it makes no difference except the fund with the higher turnover is likely to generate higher expenses because of the additional commissions being paid.

STOCK FUNDS

FUND NAME AND TELEPHONE	TYPE	AVG. ANNUAL 5-YR TOTAL RETURN (%)
Dodge & Cox Balanced 415/434-0311	G/I	13.1
Dreyfus 800/645-6561	G/I	11.9
Dreyfus 3rd Century	G/I	16.1
Fidelity Value 800/544-8888	G	16.2
Gateway Index Plus 800/354-6339	G/I	14.3
Lexington Corp. Leaders 800/526-0056	G/I	14.3
Lindner 314/727-5305	G/I	12.5
Neuberger/Berman Guardian 800/877-9700	G/I	18.8
Neuberger/Berman Manhattan	G	16.7
Neuberger/Berman Select Sectors	G	16.5
Nicholas 800/227-5987	G	17.5

Funds continued on following pages:

STOCK FUNDS (Cont'd)

Pennsylvania Mutual 800/221-4268	G	14.5
T. Rowe Price Growth/Income 800/638-5660	G/I	15.0
Safeco Equity 800/426-6730	G/I	16.8
Safeco Income	G/I	11.7
Solomon Bros. Investors 800/725-6666	G/I	13.1
Solomon Bros. Opportunity	G	13.3
Sentry 800/533-7827	G	16.1
SteinRoe Special 800/338-2550	M/G	19.0
SteinRoe Stock	G	16.8
SteinRoe Total Return	G/I	12.3
Stratton Monthly Div. Shares 800/634-5726	G/I	13.3
UMB Stock 800/422-2766	G	12.1
USAA Growth 800/531-8181	G	13.8
USAA Income	G/I	12.2
Value Line Income 800/223-0818	G/I	12.9

STOCK FUNDS (Cont'd)

Vanguard Index 500 800/662-7447	G/I	15.6
Vanguard Morgan Growth	G	15.9
Vanguard Preferred Stock	G/I	12.3
Vanguard World-U.S. Growth	G	18.8
Wellesley Income	G/I	13.5
Wellington	G/I	12.9
William Blair Growth Shares 800/742-7272	G	16.3

NOTE: S&P 500 (1988-1993) average annual return = 16.1% per year.

G = Growth; G/I = Growth/Income;   M/G = Maximum Growth

Where telephone number is not shown for a listed fund, refer to the number shown for the first listing of that particular fund family.

TABLES OF PAST PERFORMANCE ARE PROVIDED FOR INFORMATION ONLY. FUTURE RESULTS FOR ANY PARTICULAR FUND MAY BE BETTER OR WORSE THAN SHOWN.

BOND FUNDS/CORPORATE

FUND NAME AND TELEPHONE	AVERAGE MATURITY YEARS	AVG.ANNUAL 5-YEAR TOTAL RETURN (%)
AARP High Quality Bond 800/253-2277	10.9	9.9
Babson Bond L 800/422-2766	13.5	10.2
Dreyfus A Bonds Plus 800/645-6561	16.9	10.9
Fidelity Convertible Sec 800/544-8888	14.3	19.2
Fidelity Intermediate Bond	9.9	9.2
Fidelity Investment Grade Bond	13.3	10.8
Fidelity Short-Term Bond	3.2	8.6
Neuberger/Berman Ltd Mat Bond 800/877-9700	2.8	8.8
Nicholas Income 414/272-6133	7.1	9.3
T. Rowe Price New Income 800/638-5660	7.7	9.8
T. Rowe Price Short Term Bond	2.3	8.0

BOND FUNDS/CORPORATE (Cont'd)

Scudder Income 800/225-2470	11.8	10.8
Scudder Short Term Bond	3.0	9.8
SteinRoe Income 800/338-2550	10.6	10.1
Strong Short-Term Bond 800/368-1030	2.7	9.1
Vanguard Bond Market 800/662-7447	8.9	10.4
Vanguard Fixed-Income Investment Grade	17.9	12.2
Vanguard Fixed-Income Short Term	3.4	9.6

Where telephone number is not shown for a listed fund, refer to the number shown for the first listing of that particular fund family.

TABLES OF PAST PERFORMANCE ARE PROVIDED FOR INFORMATION ONLY. FUTURE RESULTS FOR ANY PARTICULAR FUND MAY BE BETTER OR WORSE THAN SHOWN.

BOND FUNDS/GOVERNMENT

FUND NAME AND TELEPHONE	AVERAGE MATURITY YEARS	AVG.ANNUAL 5-YEAR TOTAL RETURN (%)
AARP GNMA & U.S. Treasury 800/253-2277	3.6	9.8
Dreyfus 100% U.S. Treasury 800/645-6561	7.0	9.9
Dreyfus 100% U.S. Treasury Long	21.6	11.3
Dreyfus Short-Int. Government	3.1	9.5
T. Rowe Price GNMA 800/638-5660	6.8	10.2
Scudder GNMA 800/225-2470	6.2	10.3
Value Line U. S. Govt 800/223-0818	24.5	10.5
Vanguard Fixed-Income GNMA 800/662-7447	9.2	11.4
Vanguard Fixed Income Short Term	3.7	8.9
WPG Govt Securities 800/223-3332	6.0	10.5

NOTE: **Lehman Bros. Government/Corporate Bond Index** (1988-1993) average annual return = 10.7%.

BOND FUNDS/MUNICIPAL

FUND NAME AND TELEPHONE	AVERAGE MATURITY YEARS	AVG. ANNUAL 5-YEAR TOTAL RETURN (%)
Benham CA Tax-Free Int Term 800/472-3389	7.4	7.6
Calvert T/F Resrvs Ltd Term 800/368-2748	0.9	6.4
Dreyfus CA Tax-Exempt 800/645-6561	24.5	8.4
Dreyfus Intermediate Municipal	9.7	8.7
Dreyfus MA Tax-Exempt	23.3	8.9
Dreyfus Municipal	22.8	9.5
Dreyfus NY Tax-Exempt	22.9	9.1
Dupree KY Tax-Free Income 800/866-0614	12.5	9.7
Fidelity Aggressive Tax-Free 800/544-8888	21.7	10.2
Fidelity CA Tax-Free High Yield	21.7	9.4
Fidelity High Yield Tax-Free	21.0	10.1
Fidelity Insured Tax-Free	20.7	9.4

BOND FUNDS/MUNICIPAL (Cont'd)

Fidelity Limited Term Municipal	11.0	8.5
Fidelity MA Tax-Free High Yield	19.8	9.6
Fidelity MI Tax-Free High Yield	21.0	9.9
Fidelity MN Tax-Free	21.6	9.0
Fidelity Municipal	22.8	9.9
Fidelity NY Tax-Free High Yield	23.0	9.7
Fidelity NY Tax-Free Insured	22.0	9.5
Fidelity OH Tax-Free High Yield	19.9	10.0
T. Rowe Price MD Tax-Free 800/638-5660	17.7	8.9
T. Rowe Price Tax-Free High Yield	21.7	10.0
Scudder High-Yield Tax-Free 800/225-2470	13.5	10.8
Scudder MA Tax-Free	12.5	10.3
Scudder Mid-Term Tax-Free	6.3	7.6

BOND FUNDS/MUNICIPAL (Cont'd)

USAA Tax-Exempt Int. Term 800/531-8181	8.6	8.9
USAA Tax-Exempt Long-Term	21.2	10.1
USAA Tax-Exempt Short-Term	2.8	6.6
Vanguard Municipal High Yield 800/662-7447	16.9	11.0
Vanguard Municipal Intermediate Term	9.5	9.6
Vanguard Municipal Limited Term	3.0	7.5
Vanguard Municipal Short-Term	1.3	6.2

Where telephone number is not shown for a listed fund, refer to the number shown for the first listing of that particular fund family.

NOTE: Lehman Bros. Municipal Bond Index (1988-1993) average annual return = 9.8%. Total Return includes tax-exempt income as well as taxable capital gains—realized and unrealized. Also, income from funds holding bonds of a single state, i.e., Dupree KY Tax-Free Income fund, is exempt from that state's income tax.

TABLES OF PAST PERFORMANCE ARE PROVIDED FOR INFORMATION ONLY. FUTURE RESULTS FOR ANY PARTICULAR FUND MAY BE BETTER OR WORSE THAN SHOWN.

APPENDIX I

Brokerage Firms

While there is nothing like a referral from a satisfied customer, not everyone is looking for the same thing in a stockbroker. Since you can buy and sell mutual fund shares directly with the funds themselves, you only need the services of an established brokerage firm to transact buy and sell orders of individually listed stocks and bonds. As a small investor, you will pay substantially higher commission rates than a high volume trader, so make your selections carefully, with a distant time horizon in mind.

If you decide to purchase stock based on a research report from a full-service firm, do the trade with that firm. It's only fair. The cost to the low volume trader isn't that much more than what a discount broker charges, and you can expect a steady flow of information in return for your business.

For the research-it-yourselfer, on the following pages is a list of established discount brokerage firms. These firms are ranked here by the commission charged to trade 100 shares of a $50 stock (according to the **American Association of Individual Investors—AAII—1993 Guide to Discount Brokerage Firms**). Not the whole story, of course, but a chance to see how commission rates vary among firms providing otherwise similar services.

DISCOUNT BROKERAGE FIRM	COMMISSION ($) 100 shrs @ $50/share	TELEPHONE
K. Aufhauser & Co.	24.99	(800) 368-3668
Pacific Brokerage Serv.	25.00	(800) 421-8395
Brown & Company	28.00	(800) 776-6061
Bidwell & Company	29.00	(800) 547-6337
Scottscale Securities	29.00	(800) 283-1950
First Nat'l Brokerage Serv.	31.00	(800) 228-3011
St. Louis Discount Sec.	32.00	(800) 726-7401
Barry Murphy & Co.	32.50	(800) 221-2111
Marsh Block & Co.	33.24	(800) 366-1500
StockCross	33.50	(800) 225-6196
Burke Christensen & Lewis Sec.	34.00	(800) 621-0392
Lombard Institutional Brokrg.	34.00	(800) 688-3462
Seaport Securities Corp.	34.00	(800) 732-7678
Kennedy, Cabot & Co.	35.00	(800) 252-0090
Tradex Brokerage Service	35.00	(800) 522-3000
Wall Street Discount Corp.	35.00	(800) 221-7990
Waterhouse Securities	35.00	(800) 934-4410
York Securities	35.00	(800) 221-3154
Arnold Securities	35.75	(800) 328-4076
The Stock Mart	35.75	(800) 421-6563
Jack White & Company	36.00	(800) 233-3411
Recom Securities	39.00	(800) 328-8600
Baker & Company	40.00	(800) 321-1640

DISCOUNT BROKERAGE FIRMS (Cont'd):

Olde Discount Stockbrokers	40.00	(800) 872-6533
Pace Securities	40.00	(800) 221-1660
People's Securities	40.00	(800) 772-4400
Peremel & Company	40.00	(800) 666-1440
ProVest	40.00	(800) 247-2752
Royal Grimm & Davis	40.00	(800) 488-5195
Shareholder Services Corp.	40.00	(800) 582-8585
Shearman, Ralston Inc.	40.00	(800) 221-4242
Marquette de Bary Co.	42.90	(800) 221-3305
Richard Blackman & Co.	43.00	(800) 631-1635
Bull & Bear Securities	44.00	(800) 262-5800
Bruno, Stolze & Co.	45.00	(800) 899-6878
First Union Brokerage Serv.	45.00	(800) 326-4434
Freeman Welwood & Co.	45.00	(800) 729-7585
Muriel Siebert & Co. "Val. Rates"	45.00	(800) 872-0711
Securities Research Inc.	45.00	(800) 327-3156
Downstate Discount Brokrg.	46.00	(813) 586-3541
T.Rowe Price Discount Brokrg.	46.00	(800) 225-7720
Fleet Brokerage Securities	46.20	(800) 221-8210
Andrew Peck Assoc.	48.00	(800) 221-5873
S.C. Costa Company	48.00	(918) 582-0110
Spear Rees & Co.	48.00	(800) 695-4220
J.D. Seibert & Company	49.00	(800) 247-3396
Quick & Reilly	49.00	(800) 221-5220
Calvert Securities Corp.	50.00	(800) 999-3699

DISCOUNT BROKERAGE FIRMS (Cont'd):

Ichan & Co.	50.00	(800) 634-8518
Kashner Davidson Securities	50.00	(800) 678-2626
R.F. Lafferty & Co.	50.00	(800) 221-8514
Russo Securities	50.00	(718) 448-2900
Whitehall Securities Inc.	50.00	(800) 223-5023
Young, Stovall and Co.	50.00	(800) 433-5132
Voss & Co.	53.63	(800) 426-8106
Fidelity Brokerage Serv.	54.00	(800) 544-6565
Charles Schwab	55.00	(800) 442-5111
Max Ule	57.00	(800) 223-6642
Atlantic Discount Brokerage	60.00	(800) 634-4935
Aurex Financial Corp.	60.00	(800) 262-8739
Robert Thomas Securities	60.00	(800) 242-1523
Shochet Securities	63.00	(800) 327-1536
Thomas F. White & Co.	65.00	(800) 669-4483
Tuttle Securities	65.00	(800) 962-5489
First Institutional Sec. Corp.	68.00	(800) 526-7486
CoreStates Securities Corp.	70.00	(800) 222-0124
Rodecker & Co. Invest. Brkrs.	72.50	(800) 676-1848
New England Invest. Entrprss.	115.00	(800) 472-7227

Note: Rates assume "market" orders on exchange-listed stocks. Rates for O-T-C stocks could be different.

APPENDIX J

Additional Reading Material

HARD CASH was written to help the would-be investor realize that starting an investment program of mutual funds or stocks and bonds can be as easy as following a recipe in a cookbook. In-depth market knowledge and advice from a broker or financial planner is not required in order to make appropriate selections—just a little time and effort. For those who are happy to leave it at that, great. For those who now seek to increase their knowledge and understanding, the following recently released books may be useful. Please note that prices are the publishers'; shipping and handling charges are extra:

> *All About Annuities,* by Gordon K. Williamson, 237 pages, $19.95. John Wiley & Sons, 605 Third Ave., New York, N.Y. 10158-0012, (800)225-5945.

> *The All Season Investor,* by Martin J. Pring, 288 pages, $29.95. John Wiley & Sons, 605 Third Ave., New York, N.Y. 10158-0012, (800)225-5945.

> *Beating the Street,* by Peter Lynch with John Rothchild, 318 pages, $23.00. Simon & Schuster, 1230 Avenue of the Americas, New York, N.Y. 10020, (212)698-7000.

> *Break the Wall Street Rule: Outperform the Stock Market by investing as an Owner,* by Michael T. Jacobs, 243 pages, $24.95. Addison-Wesley Publishing Company, 1 Jacob Way, Reading, Mass. 01867-3999, (800)447-2226.

Additional Reading Material (Cont'd):

Dun & Bradstreet Guide to Your Investments, by Nancy
Dunnan, 394 pages, $15.00 paperback. HarperCollins
Publishers, 10 East 53rd Street, New York, N.Y.
10022, (800) 331-3761.

High Finance on a Low Budget, by Mark Skousen &
JoAnn Skousen, 257 pages, $19.95. Dearborn Financial
Publishing, 520 North Dearborn St., Chicago, Ill.
60610, (800) 621-9621.

How Mutual Funds Work, by Albert J. Fredman &
Russ Wiles, 334 pages, $15.95 paperback. New York
Institute of Finance, 2 Broadway, 5th Floor, New York,
N.Y. 10004, (800) 947-7700.

How to Profit From Reading Annual Reports, by
Richard B. Loth, 176 pages, $19.95.   Dearborn
Financial Publishing, 520 North Dearborn St., Chicago,
Ill. 60610, (800) 621-9621.

Investment Illusions, by Martin S. Fridson, 230 pages,
$24.95. John Wiley & Sons Inc., 605 Third Ave., New
York, N.Y. 10158-0012, (800) 225-5945.

Investment Psychology Explained, by Martin J. Pring,
273 pages, $24.95. John Wiley & Sons Inc., 605 Third
Ave., New York, N.Y. 10158-0012, (800) 225-5945.

*"It's a Sure Thing": A Wry Look at Investing,
Investors, and the World of Wall Street,* by Robert
Metz & George Stasen, 243 pages, $15.95. McGraw-
Hill, Inc., 1221 Avenue of the Americas, New York,
N.Y. 10020, (800) 262-4729.

Additional Reading Material (Cont'd):

Life After CDs: A Practical Guide to Safe Investing, by Michael Martin, 308 pages, $19.95 paperback. Dearborn Financial Publishing, 520 North Dearborn St., Chicago, Ill. 60610, (800) 621-9621.

Money Management Basics, by Howard Sutton and the editors of Consumer Reports Books, 216 pages, $14.95. Consumers Union, 101 Truman Ave., Yonkers, N.Y. 10703-1057, (914) 378-2000.

Moody's Handbook of Dividend Achievers, 1993 edition, $19.95. Moody's Investors Service, 99 Church Street, New York, N.Y. 10007, (212) 553-0300.

Small Stocks, Big Profits, by Gerald W. Perritt, 274 pages, $17.95 paperback. Dearborn Financial Publishing, 520 North Dearborn St., Chicago, Ill. 60610, (800) 621-9621.

Stock Picking: The 11 Best Tactics for Beating the Market, by Richard J. Maturi, 208 pages, $12.95 paperback. McGraw Hill, Inc., 1221 Avenue of the Americas, New York, N.Y. 10020, (800)262-4729.

The StreetWise Investor, by Charles L. Fahy with Sydney LeBlanc, 198 pages, $22.95. Probus Publishing, 1925 N. Clybourn Ave., Chicago, Ill. 60614, (800) 776-2871.

Terry Savage's New Money Strategies for the '90s, by Terry Savage, 559 pages, $23.00. Harper Business, 10 East 53rd St., New York, N.Y. 10022, (800) 242-7737.

Additional Reading Material (Cont'd):

The Ultimate Mutual Fund Guide, by Warren Boroson, 289 pages, $16.95 paperback. Probus Publishing, 1925 N. Clybourn Ave., Chicago, Ill. 60614, (800) 776-2871.

Value Averaging, second edition, by Michael E. Edleson, 235 pages, $22.95. International Publishing Corp., 625 N. Michign Ave., Chicago, Ill. 60611, (312) 943-7354.

Wealth: An Owner's Manual, by Michael Stolper, 266 pages, $20.00. Harper Business, 10 East 53rd St., New York, N.Y. 10022-5299, (800) 331-3761.

GLOSSARY

Bond Yield: Simply put, it's the ratio of the annual interest to the price of the bond. If the bond pays $80 per year, and your cost is $950, then the "Current Yield" is 80 / 950 = 8.42%. The "Yield-to-Maturity" calculation assumes that all interest payments will be reinvested at the coupon rate until maturity. Not too realistic, but it's the only accurate way to compare bonds. The "Yield-to-the-Call" is figured as if the bond matures on the "call" date, and pays the call price, say 103% of par. So when getting a quote, insist on the yield-to-maturity and, if callable, the yield-to-the-call. These two calculations are complicated, and require a bond yield table or a suitably programmed calculator.

Commodities (pork bellies, wheat, corn, gold, T-bills, etc.): When traded as futures contracts, allow the hedger or speculator to place a small "good faith" deposit with the "exchange," and control maybe twenty times the deposit in corn, gold, etc. until the contract expires. Used by, say, a corn producer to protect (hedge) the selling price of his future harvest, and by the speculator to leverage his capital. While the trader will always "close out" the contract before the expiration date, hopefully at a profit, it is theoretically possible for him to fail to do so, and end up with two carloads of corn on a railroad siding and a very large invoice to go with it.

Convertible: An automobile with a fold-away top, or in investments, a fixed income security (bond or preferred stock) which can be changed into common stock at a specific price. They can be found in the back of the *S&P Bond Guide*. The upside potential and the downside risk are influenced and contained by both interest rates and the price of the stock. Usually of lower quality than other debt of the company—the convertible feature being added as an inducement to buy them—they return above average yields. So the holder has the benefit of a high yield and a lower-risk-opportunity to profit if the stock takes off later on.

Distribution Rate: Where mentioned by a bond mutual fund, the percentage payout a fund may declare from the sum total of such things as bond interest, any return of principal, and any income generated by hedging strategies using options or interest rate futures. Sometimes incorrectly stated as "yield"; usually paid monthly.

Dividend: The periodic amount paid to holders of common and preferred stock, and stock mutual funds. Dividends on common stock and mutual funds are usually declared and paid quarterly. Dividends on preferred stock are fixed at the time of issue and also paid quarterly. Note—not all common stocks pay dividends. Some used to, fell on hard times, and had to stop; others never have, but are in the early stages of their growth. It's important to know the difference.

Dividend Yield: The ratio of the annual dividend to the current price of the stock. Unlike bonds, where the yield is a function of quality and maturity, stock dividends are whatever the corporation chooses to pay—considering profits, losses, and apparent shareholder loyalty. Relatively higher yields are usually found among utility stocks; lower yields among mature growth stocks; lowest or no yields among young growth stocks or stocks which have reduced or cut their dividends due to problems.

Expense Ratio: In mutual funds, management fees and expenses divided by average net assets. Most funds average about one percent. It does not include Rule 12(b)-1 fees or sales charges.

Financial Planner: Usually a self-employed, certified (by a professional association) advisor who either recommends the most suitable portfolio for a client, and charges only a service fee, or who may recommend the product (mutual fund, annuity contract, or stock portfolio) which pays the highest commission, and may or may not charge a service fee on top of that.

Guaranteed Investment Contract (GIC): Fixed income vehicle issued by insurance companies and backed by their bond portfolios. Once thought to be very safe until some insurance companies discovered junk bonds.

Interest Income: The periodic payments received by creditors (bond holders) usually semi-annually if from an individual issue, or monthly if from a bond mutual fund.

International Mutual Fund: A fund which invests in stocks issued by companies of foreign countries. Because their holdings are subject to changes in foreign currency exchange rates as well as stock markets that may be running counter to U.S. markets, they can help balance the total portfolio.

Junk Bond: Until the 1980's, the corporate bond of a company which had fallen on hard times. Downgraded by the rating services, their interest payments in doubt, if being paid at all, junk bonds were purchased only by very sophisticated investors who anticipated a turnaround or debt restructuring and eventual price recovery. By the early 80's, the term junk bond became more closly identified with brand-new issues of poorly secured debt. Issued to finance the leveraged-buy-out (LBO) craze of the era, many were purchased by out-of-their-element savings and loan corporations, insurance companies, and then-wealthy individuals.

Liquid Investment: One which can be converted to cash quickly, such as U.S. Treasury bills and money market mutual funds. However, any investment which has an active secondary market is considered liquid even if also subject to significant price swings—listed stocks, mutual funds, and most bonds.

Examples of illiquid investments are real estate, collectibles, and limited partnerships.

Load (front-end, back-end): The sales charge levied by a mutual fund, usually when purchased through a broker or financial planner. Some traditional no-load companies charge a low-load (1% to 3%) on their most popular funds to discourage their use in "market timing" programs which call for frequent switching in and out.

Net Asset Value (NAV): What the portfolio of a mutual fund is worth (market value) at a given point in time. This is usually calculated at the end of each trading day.

Prospectus: The booklet size document which explains the main features of a new stock, bond, limited partnership, or mutual fund offering. In the case of mutual funds, a prospectus is issued periodically, and it includes the investment objectives and policies, instructions for buying and redeeming shares, and an updated performance history.

Risk/Reward Ratio: Usually expressed as a decimal. For example, an analyst may forecast that ABC stock is likely to go up four points within the next six months, but in the meantime it may drop one point. The risk/reward ratio is 0.25 (1/4).

Rule 12(b)-1 Fee: The amount some mutual funds will deduct from their assets annually to pay for marketing costs. The law allows up to 1.25%. That's on top of normal management fees and any sales charges.

Rule of 72: A formula for approximating either the years needed to double your money when invested at a specific rate, or the annual rate of return needed to double your money over a specific period. For example: Given an annual rate of return of 17%, it will take about 4 years to double your money (72 / 17 = 4.24). Or if you want to double your money in 7 years, then your investments must return about 10% per year (72 / 7 = 10.28).

Stock Dividends: Instead of cash the company pays out shares of stock to its existing shareholders. Like a stock split, it has no immediate effect on the value of one's holdings—the IRS agrees and does not tax it. However, the practice does allow a company to conserve cash and still pay a "dividend."

Stock Option (index option, futures option): The right to buy (call) or sell (put) a particular stock (unit, futures contract) at a pre-determined price (striking price) for a certain period of time (up to the expiration date). They are used in many combinations (including spreads and straddles) and forms (covered or naked) by both hedgers (who own the underlying security) and speculators (who just like the leverage). While much lower than the underlying security, the price of the option moves in concert with it. In certain instances (in-the-money) a stock option may move point for point with the stock.

Stock Split: What a company does to make its common stock more marketable (easier to buy). A round lot (100 shares) of a stock trading at $50 per share goes for $5,000 plus commission. That price squeezes out the small investor who would like to add a round lot to his portfolio with two or three thousand dollars. So the company splits the stock, say, 5 for 2. Now the shares go for $20, and $2,000 plus commission buys 100 shares. The owners of shares, before the split, now own 5/2 or 2.5 times more shares worth exactly the same money. While stocks are usually split 2 for 1, 3 for 2, 5 for 2, and so forth, they may also be reverse split, say, 1 for 5. However, the idea behind a reverse split may be to take the stock out of the relm of "penny stocks" in order to affect an image change.

Stockbroker: A licensed securities salesperson, usually paid by commission,   who   is   often   made   to   choose   between recommending the best course of action for his or her client, or putting food on the table at home. Most choose the former—some choose the latter. Can you tell the difference?

Turnover: In mutual funds, the annual rate that its stocks or bonds are exchanged (traded) for other stocks or bonds. A conservative growth/income fund may average a turnover rate of 25%; an aggressive growth fund may average 300% or more.

Unit Investment Trust (UIT): A collection of bonds issued as a single security by an investment company. Not to be confused with a mutual fund, the bonds in a UIT are not traded unless forced out by a downgrade or default. While the average maturity of the trust portfolio may be, say, ten years, the maturity of the individual issues within the portfolio may vary from five to thirty years. As they mature, it's hard to reinvest small principal payouts in anything but money market funds, so the yield of the trust itself tends to suffer over time. Also, they are only available through brokers at a moderate sales charge, so they should only be considered for the long haul. Finally, the minimum purchase is usually $5,000—the same as an individual bond, but much more than most mutual funds.

Warrant: In investments, it is usually attached to a newly issued bond to make the bond more attractive for purchase. It gives the holder the right to buy a share of common stock at a specified price for a limited period of time. Sounds like a call option except that the expiration date is usually in years instead of months. Once detached when the bond is issued, the warrant will usually trade on the same exchange as the common.

INDEX

INDEX

INDEX

INDEX

INDEX

INDEX

INDEX

INDEX

INDEX

INDEX

INDEX

ORDER FORM

MAIL TO: **Strebor Publications**
P. O. Box 475
Laguna Beach, CA 92652

Please ship to me at the address below the following number of copies of *HARD CASH: A Primer for the Small Investor.* Enclosed is my check or money order in the amount of $_____ which includes $2.75 (each) shipping and handling and $0.70 (each) California sales tax *(tax applies to orders shipped to California only).*

_____ copies @ $8.95 each $_____

Shipping & handling @ $2.75 each   _____

CA. sales tax @ $0.70 each   _____

TOTAL AMOUNT   _____

Ship to:

Name_____

Address_____

City_____

State_____   Zip_____

Daytime Telephone No. (_____) _____

CREDIT CARD ORDERS 1-800-345-0096

ORDER FORM

MAIL TO: **Strebor Publications**
P. O. Box 475
Laguna Beach, CA 92652

Please ship to me at the address below the following number of copies of *How To Save Money On Just About Everything.* Enclosed is my check or money order in the amount of $_____ which includes $3.50 (each) shipping and handling and $1.00 (each) California sales tax *(tax applies to orders shipped to California only).*

_____ copies @ $12.95 each $_____

Shipping & handling @ $3.50 each   _____

CA. sales tax @ $1.00 each   _____

TOTAL AMOUNT   _____

Ship to:

Name_____

Address_____

City_____

State_____   Zip_____

Daytime Telephone No. (_____) _____

CREDIT CARD ORDERS 1-800-345-0096

ABOUT THE AUTHOR

Philip Groves is a former investment broker with fourteen years experience in all facets of the business. His clients have included experienced investors—those employing large private placement transactions, municipal bonds, and managed portfolios—as well as first-time investors just starting a mutual fund portfolio.

Prior to entering the investment community, Groves spent sixteen years in the corporate business world. During that time he held a variety of technical, training and marketing positions.